Entrepreneur.
ULTIMATE
GUIDE TO

shopify

Jason R. Rich

Entrepreneur Press®

Entrepreneur Books, Publisher
Cover Design: Andrew Welyczko
Production and Composition: Eliot House Productions

This publication is designed to provide accurate and authoritative information in regard to the subject
matter covered. It is sold with the understanding that the publisher is not engaged in rendering legal,
accounting, or other professional services. If legal advice or other expert assistance is required, the services
of a competent professional person should be sought.

Entrepreneur Books® is a registered trademark of Entrepreneur Media, Inc.

Library of Congress Cataloging-in-Publication Data
Names: Rich, Jason R., author.
Title: Ultimate guide to shopify / by Jason R. Rich.
Description: Irvine : Entrepreneur Press, 2022. | Series: Entrepreneur ultimate guides | Includes index.
Identifiers: LCCN 2022030301 (print) | LCCN 2022030302 (ebook) | ISBN 9781642011494 (trade
    paperback) | ISBN 9781613084618 (epub)
Subjects: LCSH: Electronic commerce. | Internet marketing. | Business enterprises—Computer
    networks.
Classification: LCC HF5548.32 .E583 2022 (print) | LCC HF5548.32 (ebook) | DDC 658.8—dc23/
    eng/20220805
LC record available at https://lccn.loc.gov/2022030301
LC ebook record available at https://lccn.loc.gov/2022030302

Printed in the United States of America

25 24 23 22   10 9 8 7 6 5 4 3 2 1

Contents

CHAPTER **9**
Top-Notch Customer Service Is Essential **147**

CHAPTER **10**
Fulfilling Your Orders **159**

CHAPTER **11**
Consider Buying an Existing Online Business **171**

Preface

It used to be that if you wanted to start a business selling products to customers, you needed to open a brick-and-mortar retail store. This represented a huge commitment in time and money, not to mention significant risk. Operating a traditional retail store also meant catering to a group of customers from a narrow geographic area while competing with mass-market superstores. In addition to maintaining regular business hours, staffing the store with employees, and typically being required to sign a long-term lease for retail space, if you made any wrong decisions, it could easily lead to the business failing and personal financial ruin.

Now, thanks to the internet, just about anyone can start an online business. An *ecommerce business* can be operated from virtually anywhere (if an internet connection is available), and just about anything that could be sold at retail can be sold online. Most important, you face significantly lower startup costs, less of a time commitment, and far less risk.

In fact, with today's technology, you could theoretically create and launch an online business in days or weeks—not months—and depending on what you plan to sell, the startup costs might be in the hundreds or thousands of dollars, as opposed to the hundreds *of* thousands of dollars (or more) needed to open a traditional retail store.

Ecommerce platform Shopify published a report in January 2022 titled "The Future of Commerce Trend Report: 2022," which noted that businesses have been forced to deal with more change in the past two years than in the previous 20. For the ecommerce business operator, this represents a potential opportunity, because more consumers than ever are now willing and able to shop online.

However, Shopify's report also noted that many challenges and changes still lie ahead, especially when it comes to product shortages, increased shipping times and costs, and higher online advertising costs. It stressed the importance of not just creating a website to sell products, but to build an interactive online community for your customers. This can be done using tools offered by Shopify, as well as various social media platforms. This trend is being referred to as "social commerce," as opposed to "ecommerce."

One of many important lessons that can be learned from this report is that "People are more willing than ever to buy from brands that resonate with them because of geography, company values, or sustainability." This makes it more important than ever for an online business operator to build their brand, company, and products around a strong, relatable, and attention-grabbing story that target customers will relate to. We will explore this concept in later chapters of the book. For example, in Chapter 5 "Creating Your Online Store," the concept of developing a brand around your business is explained.

Some Benefits to Operating an Online Business

People of all ages (starting as young as their early teens), from all walks of life, and from all over the world have discovered that operating an ecommerce business can be a highly lucrative part-time or full-time business opportunity with virtually limitless potential. Starting an online business allows you to become your own boss, set your own work schedule, work from your home (or an office), and potentially reach a global audience.

Unlike a traditional retail store, an ecommerce business is available to customers 24 hours a day, 7 days a week, regardless of where they're located (provided you're willing and able to ship your physical products to customers located outside your home country).

By 2024, eMarketer and Insider Intelligence predict that ecommerce sales worldwide will reach $6.7 trillion. According to Shopify, back in 2019 online purchases represented just 13.6 percent of all product purchases by consumers, but by 2021 the figure had reached 19.5 percent. By 2024, it's predicted to reach at least 21.8 percent. While online purchasing continues to be used by more and more U.S. consumers, this is a global phenomenon. In 2020, Latin America had the highest growth of retail ecommerce sales, followed by North America, Europe, and Asia.

Out of all the countries on earth, however, China represents the largest pool of consumers who shop online. As of 2022, Chinese consumers were responsible for $2.8 trillion in online sales, compared to the U.S., which was responsible for $843 billion.

Shopify predicts that by 2024, there will be more than 2.14 billion consumers worldwide who regularly shop online. Obviously, not all these people will be a prospective customer for your business, but even a tiny percentage of them represents a huge potential market that your website can appeal to.

Ecommerce Offers Tremendous Opportunity

As an online business operator, it'll be your responsibility to identify a niche target audience for your products out of the ever-growing population that's willing and able to shop online and then learn how to reach that audience to drive them to your website. It'll then be your job to convert visitors to your website into paying customers and later convert those customers into repeat customers.

A traditional website conveys information to a visitor through text, photos, video, graphics, animations, sound, and other multimedia content. An *ecommerce website* does much the same thing, but its purpose is to showcase products for potential customers and then offer an interactive shopping cart that allows them to quickly select and pay for them using a credit card, debit card, or electronic payment service. An ecommerce website can be accessed through an internet-connected desktop computer, laptop, smartphone, tablet, and sometimes other devices, such as a smart watch, smart speaker, or smart TV.

As an up-and-coming ecommerce business operator, it's essential to keep up-to-date on the latest consumer and technology trends. For example, mobile ecommerce continues to experience major growth worldwide. This means that more and more consumers are doing their online shopping from mobile devices, such as smartphones and tablets. At least through 2024, business research firm Insider Intelligence forecasts that the percentage of consumers who shop online using their mobile devices will increase at a 25.5 percent compound annual rate.

Virtually any physical product traditionally sold in a retail store can also be sold online. In addition, an ecommerce website can be used to sell services or digital products (ebooks, audiobooks, videos, NFTs, software, mobile apps, etc.) that get purchased and downloaded by the customer, as opposed to physical products that get shipped to them through the mail.

As you'll discover shortly, however, while just about anything can be sold online by a small ecommerce business operator, not everything will generate sales and allow them to earn a profit. Before you invest the time, effort, and money required to launch an online business, it's essential that you focus carefully on what you'll be selling, who you'll be selling to, what competition already exists, and whether your product ideas are viable. That's the focus of Chapter 3, "What Can Be Sold Online."

What makes starting and operating an ecommerce business so attractive to so many people is that if you rely on an *ecommerce turnkey solution*, you don't need to become a tech-savvy website designer or programmer to create a professional-looking and highly functional ecommerce website that will appeal to your target audience. If you know how to use email, navigate the web, and use a word processor, you already have the basic skill set you need to create and operate an online business.

Shopify Is a Powerful Ecommerce Turnkey Solution

As the name suggests, an *ecommerce turnkey solution* is a set of tools available to online business operators that were created by programmers, website designers, graphic artists, and other professionals to make starting an ecommerce website easy even for nontechnical people. Using an ecommerce website template (or "theme"), an online business operator simply needs to add details and artwork related to their products and company, often using a drag-and-drop user interface, to create a professional and easy-to-use website, with no programming required.

Many companies now offer ecommerce turnkey solutions to online business operators and entrepreneurs. To get started with one of them requires a very small financial investment and no long-term commitment. How much time it'll take you to create and launch your ecommerce site will vary greatly, however, depending on a wide range of factors that we'll be exploring shortly. However, creating and operating this type of business involves far less risk than opening and operating a traditional retail store.

What Is Shopify?

Originally launched in 2006, Shopify has become one of the world's most popular and successful ecommerce turnkey solutions, offering products, services, and support to more than 1.75 million online business operators of all sizes from about 175 countries. Shopify offers the tools and resources most business operators need to create, launch, market, and manage a successful ecommerce business. Most of these tools and services are highly customizable and relatively easy to use, with a minimal learning curve associated with them. A startup ecommerce business operator can begin using the Shopify platform for as little as $29 per month (as of 2022). For all these reasons, Shopify is considered one of the world's leading ecommerce platforms, with a U.S. market share of 23 percent as of the end of 2021.

However, while Shopify is the primary focus of *Ultimate Guide to Shopify*, it's important to understand that this service is not your only option, and that the decision about which ecommerce turnkey solution you choose should be based on a wide range of factors, such as what you'll be selling, who you'll be selling to, the scalability you'll need as your business grows, your level of technical expertise, and the collection of tools and pricing that you require.

You should also understand that the author and publisher of the *Ultimate Guide to Shopify* are in no way affiliated with Shopify. The goal of this book is to offer you an unbiased resource that will include a comprehensive introduction to the Shopify platform and eventually help you launch a successful online business. Keep in mind that technology and consumer buying habits change continuously, and that the Shopify platform continues to evolve and expand, with updates as well as new products and services designed to give online business operators the tools they need to manage a successful ecommerce business.

Moving forward, know that people from all walks of life have operated and continue to run successful ecommerce businesses using the Shopify platform. But the more knowledge, education, and experience you have, whether it's from running a traditional business or an online business, the bigger advantage you'll have over your competition. As you'll see, simply creating a professional-looking website that nicely showcases your products is just one piece of the ecommerce puzzle you'll need to master.

Operating a successful online business will require you to juggle a wide range of tasks: bookkeeping, sales, inventory management, customer service, writing/editing, advertising, marketing, promotions, product photography, product shipping, and public relations. You'll also need to become an expert on whatever it is you plan to sell and learn how to pinpoint, and successfully reach, your niche target audience.

Sure, you'll be able to learn some of these skills as you go. You can also hire experts to help you along the way. But regardless of what you plan to sell, or whom you plan to sell it to, it's essential to establish a stable foundation for your online business. Thus, the stronger your skill set is at the start, the greater your chances of success will be.

10 Common Issues Related to Running an Online Business

As you begin your quest to become an ecommerce entrepreneur and launch your own online business, it's essential to start off with realistic expectations. The following are just some of the misconceptions people commonly have when they decide to start a business online:

1. Operating an ecommerce business is a get-rich-quick scheme. It's not!
2. Even if you choose the perfect products/services to sell and create an amazing website, just publishing a website online will not automatically lead to sales, profits, and great wealth. One of the costliest aspects of running an online business (and one that requires a significant time commitment as well) is advertising, marketing, and promoting your business to generate a steady flow of traffic (visitors) to your website.
3. Realistically, it could take weeks, months, or even a year (possibly longer) before your online business becomes profitable.
4. Regardless of what you choose to sell or who you identify as your target audience, you're going to have a lot of competition from other businesses, both brick-and-mortar and online.
5. Operating an ecommerce business is an actual business (not a hobby). It will require a significant time and financial commitment, but you should not quit your existing job until you know your new business can generate the profit needed to sustain itself and provide you with a salary. As a legal business entity, you will need to pay taxes and maintain accurate financial records.

6. Not all online businesses succeed. In fact, many fail. By reading this book, however, you will learn how to avoid many of the most common pitfalls people encounter as they launch and begin operating an ecommerce business using the Shopify platform.

7. While the Shopify platform is powerful, constantly evolving, and widely used, it may not be the right choice for your specific business. No single solution or set of tools is ideal for everyone. Once you determine what you want to sell and who your target audience will be, it's your job to research the tools that are best suited to your needs, budget, and skill set.

8. Choosing to use the Shopify platform will not replace the need for you to make your own business decisions. There will be plenty of important decisions to make upfront and then moving forward. Mistakes could become time-consuming and costly, and result in the failure of your operation in the long run. As with any business, creating a proper business plan, doing plenty of research, and making sure you don't cut necessary corners to save time and money will be essential.

9. Online businesses run themselves. No! This is a common misconception! You will need to constantly update and manage your website, promote and advertise your business, keep your customers happy, and handle a wide range of responsibilities that will ensure your business operates smoothly. While you can set your own schedule and potentially run your online business on a part-time basis, it will never become a "self-running" or "fully automated" venture.

10. You can't sell low-cost, imported junk to customers at a high profit margin and expect to grow a profitable business. Whether it's through social media, product ratings/reviews, business ratings/reviews, or word-of-mouth, if you attempt to rip off consumers, misrepresent or lie about your products, or mislead your customers in any way, your reputation will quickly be tarnished, and you'll see your sales grind to a halt. As a small business operator, you should offer your customers top-quality products, top-notch customer service, and an overall quick-and-easy online shopping experience.

It All Starts with a Great Idea!

To become a successful ecommerce entrepreneur, you need a great idea regarding what you want to sell and whom you want to sell it to. As you'll discover, you need to come up with one or more products or services that are in demand, have a decent profit margin, are easily sourced or manufactured, and do not have an insane amount of competition.

Ideally, you also want evergreen products that are not seasonal or fad-based, and that have a growing niche customer base that you can easily and affordably identify and reach.

In other words, as a small, independent online business operator, you cannot compete with Target, Walmart, Costco, Amazon, mall chain stores, popular franchises, or any other mass-market seller when it comes to commonly used products or services. Your best chance for success lies in selling unique or unusual items to a niche audience that you can easily target with your marketing efforts.

Once you have identified both the products and/or services to sell and the target audience you plan to sell them to, *only then* should you start designing and planning your ecommerce website. As one of the world's leading ecommerce platforms, there's a good chance that Shopify will provide the tools and services you need both now and in the future, which is why reading the *Ultimate Guide to Shopify* is a good first step toward getting your online business started.

In addition to helping you quickly get acquainted with the Shopify platform, this book includes 10 exclusive in-depth interviews with Shopify experts and experienced online business operators who have achieved success using Shopify. In these interviews, you'll discover real-world advice and strategies that will help you achieve success and learn how to avoid common mistakes that other ecommerce entrepreneurs have made before you.

Consider these experts to be your mentors. While you'll likely never meet or interact with them in person, you can still learn a lot from their experiences as you move forward with your own business venture. In addition to these interviews, this book is full of helpful tips, free (and low-cost) resources, and detailed advice that'll help you navigate the often-overwhelming world of ecommerce.

Especially as the world's population learns how to navigate the post–COVID-19 landscape, the ongoing reliance people have developed on online shopping over the past few years will not diminish anytime soon. If you can provide your customers with an online shopping experience that's quick, easy, risk-free, and competitive on price, while offering a superior customer-service experience, top-quality products, and fast shipping, you'll be well on your way to building a viable and profitable ecommerce business using the tools offered by Shopify.

The primary goal of the *Ultimate Guide to Shopify* is to help you navigate the road ahead, as you develop and flesh out the idea for your online business and then invest the time, energy, money, and resources needed to make it a reality and succeed using the Shopify platform.

After reading this book, you should be able to determine whether your idea is viable, understand the steps you need to take to create and manage a successful ecommerce website, determine what additional help you may need, and recognize how Shopify can help you save time and money as you get your business venture off the ground.

CHAPTER 1

Introduction to Shopify

If you have one or more products you wish to sell online, you'll need to create a website with ecommerce capabilities, which means that in addition to containing a description and photos of the products being sold, the website will need to be integrated with a shopping cart function, giving it the ability to accept orders and process payments.

You have a wide range of options when it comes to creating a professional-looking ecommerce website with all the features and functionality you'll need. The most costly and complicated option is to create and program a website from scratch, launch it online, and then promote it to your potential audience. This requires you to have web programming and graphic design skills, not to mention the wherewithal to operate a business.

An Ecommerce Turnkey Solution Offers an Easy Way to Launch Your Online Business

A more cost-effective approach is to take advantage of an ecommerce turnkey solution, using a well-established and reputable service provider. This option requires no programming whatsoever, and while some basic graphic design skills will be useful, they're not essential. When you use an ecommerce turnkey solution, all the tools you need to create, publish, and manage your ecommerce website are provided to you via an online service. All you need to do is pick a template (or theme) for your website, add the content you need (often using drag-and-drop functionality), and then use the premade tools to publish and manage your site.

Because you're customizing a preexisting website template that was designed by professional programmers and graphic artists, all you need to do is supply the assets that will be featured on your website, such as your company logo, product descriptions, and product photos. (We will discuss how to do this in Chapter 5, "Creating Your Online Store.") You will typically have a wide selection of templates/themes to choose from, so you should choose one that complements what you're selling and to whom you're selling it.

In most cases, you'll also have access to a vast array of optional features and functions (in the form of apps) that you can add to your ecommerce website (again, with no programming required). You'll need to look these options over and decide which of them you want to use—remembering to keep your website as user-friendly and clutter-free as possible.

When creating your ecommerce website, every decision should be made with your intended customers in mind. Remember that your website visitors will have a very short attention span, so if they can't find what they want quickly, they will simply click away from your site and probably never return.

Thus, your goal should always be to provide the fastest, easiest, most convenient, and most reliable shopping experience possible—without including anything that could distract or confuse visitors to your website. The more you know the intended target audience for your products and the better you understand their shopping habits and needs, the easier it'll be to create a website that truly caters to them.

It's important to understand that no single formula, website design, or sales approach works for all products being sold to all customers. Your products need to be carefully curated, and when someone visits your website, everything they see, hear, and experience must cater specifically to their wants and needs.

To accomplish this, you must pinpoint the target audience for your products, understand the online shopping habits of this niche audience, and then cater every aspect of your website's design to them by choosing the most appropriate ecommerce turnkey solution and using the tools they offer to their utmost advantage.

You Have Numerous Ecommerce Turnkey Solution Options

Shopify is a proven ecommerce platform that's relatively easy-to-use, affordable, scalable, and constantly evolving to offer online sellers the tools and functions they need to capitalize on the latest consumer online buying trends, while ensuring compatibility with all the latest computers, web browsers, smartphones, and tablets. Shopify offers everything you need to design, publish, and manage your ecommerce business for a flat monthly fee that ranges between $29 and $299, depending on the service plan you select.

Shopify is not your only option, however, when it comes to choosing an ecommerce turnkey solution. Depending on what you're selling, whom you'll be selling to, your level of comfort with technology, and the features and functions you need to incorporate into your website, many other ecommerce turnkey solutions are available to you as an online seller. Some of these include:

- *Etsy*: www.etsy.com/sell?ref=ftr
- *GoDaddy*: www.godaddy.com/websites/online-store
- *Network Solutions*: www.networksolutions.com/website/e-commerce-website-builder
- *Square Online*: https://squareup.com/us/en/online-store
- *Web.com*: https://www.web.com/website-builder-landing
- *Wix eCommerce*: https://www.wix.com/ecommerce/website
- *WordPress*: https://wordpress.org

Each of these services offers a slightly different collection of features, functions, and tools, along with its own selection of templates or themes. Before choosing a platform, it's important to determine your objectives, and to decide what features and functionality your website will need on the front and back end.

Etsy, for example, is an online shopping community designed specifically for selling handcrafted items, and it provides an easy way to launch an online store if you're a painter, sculptor, jewelry maker, knitter, or other type of crafter. The rest of the services listed above offer tools for anyone to sell just about anything online—whether you have one product or a vast catalog of products with each item available in a variety of sizes and colors.

10 Things to Look for When Choosing an Ecommerce Turnkey Solution

As you're evaluating what each platform offers to online merchants and business operators, pay attention to the following 10 issues:

1. How long the service has been operating online and what its reputation is among sellers and consumers
2. The features and functions offered for designing, publishing, and managing all aspects of your online business
3. How easy the service and its tools are to use, both for you (the online merchant) and your customers. If, say, the checkout process takes too long or is too complicated, you'll wind up losing business.
4. The number and quality of the themes or templates you can choose from. Your website must look professional and have zero bugs, and you must be able to customize whichever template or theme you choose in order to properly brand your business and showcase your products.
5. The level of customer service and support offered by the ecommerce platform (and third-party experts), so that when you run into any type of question or technical issue, you can get it answered or resolved quickly
6. The upfront and ongoing fees you'll be charged per month and/or per sale, including all payment processing fees

7. The level of technical know-how needed to use the service and the learning curve associated with it

8. The ability to scale your website as your business grows, without having to switch platforms

9. The security and privacy tools and features automatically included in the platform

10. The assurance that your website will support all hardware platforms and web browsers and will adapt automatically to whatever hardware or software your visitors are using. Your site's shopping experience should be flawless, whether someone is using a full-size computer monitor, a tablet, or their smartphone to purchase your products.

The best way to determine which ecommerce platform is best for your business is to do your research. Visit a handful of popular platforms, review the services they offer, and look at some sample websites that run on those platforms. Next, determine who your top competitors will be once you launch your business, and try to determine what ecommerce platform they are using.

When visiting the websites of your potential competitors, do so as a customer and make a purchase. As you go through the purchasing process, pay attention to its strengths and weaknesses. What does each competitor's website do well? What problems or questions do you encounter as a customer? What ways could you improve on the experience with your own website? Doing this will help you define the consumer experience you're striving to achieve with your own website and help you narrow down your search for an ecommerce turnkey solution that offers the tools to provide that experience, as well as a professional appearance to every aspect of the site.

Shopify Offers Many Options to Business Operators

As we delve deeper into Shopify's offerings, you'll see that this platform not only offers scalable ecommerce solutions suitable for any size business, but also a vast selection of tools and resources to help you build your brand; create an online presence; manage your store; and establish the foundation for you to sell via your website, through a Shopify Buy Button incorporated into your social media posts, in person, or through Google Shopping, Walmart Marketplace, eBay, and other platforms.

Shopify also provides integrated tools to help you market and promote your business through email, online advertising, and online chats/text messaging, as well as tools to handle the back end of your business, such as payment processing, shipping, inventory management, and handling returns and refunds. Shopify also supplies you with comprehensive and real-time analytics that allow you to track every aspect of your business, including the interactions people have while using your website.

DROPSHIPPING IS AN OPTION, BUT IT MIGHT NOT BE A GREAT ONE

You also have the option to quickly set up relationships with dropshippers and then create a website to sell products that you never actually take possession of. In other words, you can sell products online and have a third-party dropshipper handle all the order fulfillment and inventory management—for a fee.

Creating an ecommerce business using the dropshipping model is possible with Shopify, but as you'll discover, it's not always the wisest route, especially if you're hoping for long-term success as an online business. Dropshipping requires you to rely heavily on one or more third parties to maintain inventory and fulfill your orders. Should something go wrong, you have little control over rectifying the situation and being able to make your customers happy.

Plus, if you sell products that are being shipped directly from China or another distant country, your customers will often place an order thinking it will be shipped and arrive within a few business days, only to discover it will instead take four to six weeks. This often results in canceled orders and can earn your business a negative reputation, leading to unfavorable ratings and reviews.

For these and other reasons that will be explored later in this book (see Chapter 3, "What Can Be Sold Online"), building an ecommerce business using a pure dropshipping model is seldom the best approach, and is therefore not one that we will spend much time on. Most of this book's focus is on choosing the best products to sell online, determining and getting to know the target audience for those items, and then using Shopify to create the best possible ecommerce website. Another major focus is on helping you market, advertise, and promote your business through a cost-effective, well-planned, multifaceted approach, as well as to help you provide the best possible customer service.

Properly handling every aspect of planning, creating, publishing, managing, marketing, and customer service for your ecommerce business is essential. If you try to cut any corners or skip putting the necessary time, money, and resources into one or more of these areas, your chances of failure increase exponentially.

The good news is that you don't have to accomplish all that on your own. Whenever you encounter something you don't yet have the knowledge, skill set, or experience to handle, you have plenty of resources available to you (including individual Shopify Experts you can hire on a per-hour or per-project basis), which, if used correctly, will greatly improve your chances of success.

Establish Realistic Goals for Your Business

While it's true that just about any type of product can be sold online, as a startup ecommerce business, you need to be very selective about what products you choose to sell. Chapter 3, "What Can Be Sold Online," will help you pick the perfect products to sell, based on your ability to reach the target audience for those products, the existing competition, and the resources you have available.

Whatever you choose to sell, however, remember that starting an online business is not a get-rich-quick scheme. Realistically, it could take several months (if not longer) for you to begin generating a steady flow of traffic to your website. That traffic then needs to be successfully converted into paying customers—and enough of them to turn a profit.

Again, there's no single formula to follow that'll guarantee your success. However, you *can* follow proven steps to establish and manage your business correctly and avoid the most common pitfalls that could lead to costly mistakes or even the demise of your business. It all comes down to choosing the best products to sell, creating the best possible ecommerce website using the tools offered by Shopify, pinpointing your target audience, and learning how to successfully market your products to that audience while maintaining a positive online reputation.

Keep in mind that while you can theoretically create an ecommerce website and establish an online business presence in a matter of days for a very low startup cost, many other steps are required to establish the foundation for your business: choose what you'll sell, get to know your audience, create the assets for your website (i.e., the content), customize the website theme or template, develop a marketing plan, set up your bookkeeping tools, establish your inventory, and get ready to start fulfilling orders. You can easily invest several weeks or months (working part time or full time) before you're ready to publish your site online and begin welcoming visitors.

Also remember that you'll have other startup costs, above whatever you'll need to spend to create your website using Shopify. You'll need to have the finances in place to advertise, promote, and market your business on an ongoing basis (before it begins to generate any revenue or profit) to drive a steady flow of traffic to your site.

How much you'll need to cover your startup costs and handle the site's advertising, marketing, and promotion will vary greatly, based on several factors that we'll delve into shortly in Chapter 8. For now, just keep in mind that the base $29 per month startup cost to use Shopify is very misleading in terms of what it'll cost you to get your business off the ground. You could easily spend several thousand dollars (or much more) during the startup phase of your business.

Avoid the Most Common Misconception About Operating an Online-Based Business

Without a doubt, the most common misconception related to starting an online ecommerce business is that if you invest just a few days to create a website and publish it online, people will automatically (and magically) discover your business and begin shopping from your site. Unfortunately, nothing could be further from the truth.

As you'll discover, you must complete numerous steps before you're ready to start accepting orders, and many of these steps have multiple subtasks that must be completed as well. Then, once your business is online and operational, it will require a significant and ongoing time investment from you: interacting with potential and existing customers, fulfilling orders, managing the website, handling customer-service issues, and juggling the other responsibilities associated with running a business (such as bookkeeping, inventory management, and marketing your business).

In every sense of the word, running an ecommerce business carries many of the same responsibilities (and requires the same core knowledge and skill set) as running any other type of business. From a technology standpoint, if you know how to do word processing and navigate the internet, you have what it takes to use the tools provided by Shopify, but you will need to tap many other skills and juggle many responsibilities to achieve success as an online business operator.

Many of the skills and the knowledge you'll need to run your business can be acquired as you go. However, the more experience you have running any type of business in the real world, and the more proficient you are at using social media and handling tasks like bookkeeping, the easier time you'll have getting your business up and running. As for any skills you're lacking, consider hiring specialized freelance help to provide the assistance you need to avoid making costly mistakes.

The World of Ecommerce Is Looking Brighter Than Ever Before

The startup costs for an online business continue to be significantly lower (and carry far less risk) than launching a traditional brick-and-mortar retail business, and more consumers than ever are shopping online—to the tune of a projected $5.55 trillion worldwide (including $875 billion in the U.S. alone) in 2022, according to research from Shopify.

According to dropshipping app company Oberlo, 27.2 percent of the world's population are considered online shoppers as of 2021, and online shopping accounts for more than 18 percent of the world's retail sales. It's expected that this will grow to 22 percent of the world's sales by the end of 2023.

With so many powerful tools at your disposal, and services like Shopify making it so easy to establish and manage an ecommerce business, there has never been a better time to launch your online business venture, provided that you do the proper research and acquire the right knowledge and skills before you start. The information in this book, including the advice you'll receive from online business operators and experts, will serve as a reliable roadmap to help you build a strong foundation for success.

As you move forward, start kicking around ideas for what you want to sell, to whom you want to sell it, what you want your ecommerce website to look like, and what website functionality you'll need to create the ideal shopping experience for your customers. With these thoughts in mind, the next chapter will help you learn more about what the Shopify platform offers and how to start using it.

Then, once you understand what's possible with Shopify, we'll focus on your business: choosing the best products to sell; pinpointing your target audience; establishing your business; learning how to market, advertise, and promote your business; finding the expert help you need; providing superior customer service; and focusing on proven strategies for fulfilling your orders in a way that will make your customers happy (and allow you to earn a profit).

SHOPIFY EXPERT

Darrell Williams
Transform a Shopify Store into a Profitable Business

Before growth marketing expert Darrell Williams started San Francisco–based Growth Hack Guides (https://growthhackguides.com), he worked for startups and digital marketing agencies at the senior leadership level. During his tenure at Shopify digital advertising agency BVA (Brand Value Accelerator), he helped multiple Shopify-based business operators launch, optimize, and scale their business ventures.

Williams created Growth Hack Guides (an online-based training program) to help aspiring entrepreneurs realize the path to success is not as hard as they might think. He believes that launching and scaling an online business becomes easier with expert guidance. This philosophy also inspired him to share his knowledge and advice through the interview you're about to read.

Q: *If someone wants to launch an online business, why is Shopify the platform they should use?*

Shopify offers a lot of different customization options and plug-ins, so it's much more versatile than many other ecommerce turnkey solutions.

It's also a more manageable platform to use, especially for startup business operators who don't know a lot about ecommerce or coding. If you happen to know how to code, Shopify is developer-friendly and offers advanced and robust tools that can give experienced online business operators much more control over every aspect of their website.

Q: *One of the things that sets Shopify apart is the existence of the Shopify Experts network. Is this a resource that all startups should rely on?*

Very few people have all the knowledge, experience, and skills needed to handle all aspects of establishing, designing, launching, managing, and promoting an ecommerce business.

For this reason, I strongly recommend that people determine their shortcomings and then seek out experts to help them along the way. The specialists who are registered with the Shopify Experts network have a high level of expertise and experience. The specialist can help startups take advantage of the more advanced functionality offered by Shopify.

Experts can help you understand product differentiation and how to create a recognizable brand around your business. However, when it comes to selling online, what you have to focus on once you have site visitors to your store is *conversion rate*, which is the percentage of visitors to your website that become paying customers.

Q: *What should people understand about the startup costs associated with launching a Shopify-based business?*

Using the Shopify platform requires a minimal startup cost. However, you may need to hire a graphic designer to create your company logo and then hire a professional photographer to take your product images.

In addition, a lawyer and an accountant are helpful to establish your legal business entity and bookkeeping. Then you'll likely have manufacturing or inventory costs associated with your products.

To acquire site traffic, I highly recommend hiring an SEO (search engine optimization) professional first to start generating sales from search engines. By hiring an SEO professional, you can learn which keywords people type in to find your products. Then, once you have established search engine traffic, hire a PPC (pay per click) specialist to utilize the keyword data to run ads on Google. Then turn your attention to hiring a social media specialist.

As you can see, the costs start to compound, but if you tackle each stage in the order I suggest, your sales should start to compound as well.

Q: *Do you have any advice on how to choose what products to sell online or the number of products an online store should start off selling?*

As a rule of thumb, I would advise people to start with no more than 10 products. You want to be selective when choosing what you'll be selling and do research in advance to determine the demand.

The more you understand about your target audience, the easier it'll be to diversify your products. You'll also have an easier time reaching a niche audience with your advertising and marketing.

In the early stages, you can't cast too wide of a net. Once your business launches, you'll want to study the analytics regularly to make sure you fully understand who your customers are and what their level of engagement is when they visit each page or section of your website.

Q: *What would you say is the biggest misconception people have when they're first starting a Shopify-based ecommerce business?*

The biggest misconception I see repeatedly is that people think if they create an ecommerce store, buyers will automatically discover their store and begin buying immediately.

There is also this misconception that once you do gain a customer, they'll become a repeat customer. You'll need to take steps to earn repeat business. One sale does not automatically equate to three more from that person in the future.

If your business model depends on you earning repeat business from customers, you need to offer a great product, an easy shopping experience, and superior customer service.

I recommend learning how to use an email marketing strategy to help generate repeat business and how to leverage email to boost your AOV (average order value).

Q: *What are some of the ways an ecommerce business can use email as a marketing tool?*

First and foremost, you have a lot of email marketing platforms at your disposal. Choose one that offers advanced customization options, but that's relatively easy to use. For example, I often recommend a service called ConvertKit [https://convertkit.com] to my clients. It's a low-cost email marketing tool that is ideal for startup ecommerce businesses with a few hundred subscribers. Still, it can quickly grow with your business once you have thousands or tens of thousands of subscribers.

The secret sauce with email marketing is creating different segmented email lists and focusing on the quality of content within your emails to your list. In addition, ensure your emails are easy to read quickly and include time-sensitive CTAs (calls to action) and provide incentives that the reader will perceive as valuable.

Always maintain an open dialogue with your customers, and make sure your emails are not perceived as annoying or intrusive. When it comes to using email marketing as a sales tool to generate business or repeat business, there is no set rule in terms of how frequently you should be sending out emails. A lot depends on what you're selling, to whom you're selling, and the approach you take with your email content.

Be careful that you don't send emails too frequently or that the contents of your emails only offer a strong sales message without including information the recipients will perceive as informative. It's essential to gauge your audience and test your email campaigns, especially as you're learning about your audience and doing your best to cater to them.

Based on my experience, if you're trying to reach consumers, email marketing works very well when the emails are sent midweek and late in the afternoon. However, you'll often see less success if emails are sent on weekends or at the beginning of a week.

Remember that many people will be reading your emails from mobile devices, so format your emails to accommodate a smaller screen.

Q: *In your opinion, what are some of the most essential core skills someone should have as they launch their ecommerce business using the Shopify platform?*

I believe in the importance of understanding SEO, as well as how to conduct CRO (conversion rate optimization) analysis, running PPC ads as soon as you launch your business. You can learn these skills or hire experts to help you, but it is critical to understand your acquisition strategy. It's also essential to understand the nuances of content creation. For example, when you launch a Shopify store, every aspect of your website should aim to educate your visitors about what you're selling, in a way that'll quickly convert those people into paying customers.

Q: *Realistically, how long will it take for someone to come up with an idea for an ecommerce business and then launch it successfully?*

There is no set timeline that works for every business. The advice I offer is to never rush any aspect of the process. Take your time. Test every part of your website, invest the time you need to create your content, do your research, and learn about your products and target customers.

Make sure every aspect of your website is easy to use and navigate, that everything works, that it contains nothing misleading or distracting, and that you proofread everything carefully. One of the first things you should do is create **SMART** goals. Setting goals is too vague. **SMART** goals are **S**pecific, **M**easurable, **A**ttainable, **R**ealistic, and **T**ime-based.

I am a firm believer that every ecommerce business should have a brand that resonates with the target customer. So start at why and not what. Everyone will know what you sell, but the key is focusing on why they should buy from you specifically.

Here is one last piece of advice that is very important. Since ecommerce stores use several images, make sure to use JPEG or WEBP image file formats. Also be sure to add image compression and an appropriate descriptive file name, caption, and metadata to each image when incorporating it into your website. In terms of scheduling and setting a time frame to launch your business, in most cases, you can go live with a new store in three to six weeks.

CHAPTER 2

Methods of Selling Online

One of the reasons so many entrepreneurs turn to Shopify to meet their ecommerce needs is that the platform offers numerous ways to sell products—above and beyond creating and managing an ecommerce website.

In fact, using its various tools, Shopify has already processed more than 2.5 billion orders (with more than 300 million of them going through Shopify Checkout). This represents more than $100 billion in sales.

What's great about using Shopify is that all the different selling options work seamlessly together, so while you may be selling products on your company's existing website, a separate ecommerce website, your blog, an email marketing campaign, social media, and/or other online retailers like eBay, Amazon, or Walmart Marketplace, everything can be managed from one place.

Furthermore, if you already operate a retail store, you have opportunities to sell to your customers in person. If you choose to use them, Shopify can still supply the tools you need to process payment transactions, manage inventory, and handle other business-related tasks.

Best of all, as your business grows, Shopify's tools and services will scale accordingly. Plus, as consumers' online buying patterns and ecommerce trends change, you can be confident that Shopify (and the third-party plugs-ins available for it) will evolve along with them to ensure you're always able to offer the features and functionality your customers expect, helping you stay competitive. Consumers now use computers, smartphones, tablets, smart watches, and smart speakers to shop online, but in the not-too-distant future, they may be using VR and AR devices like smart eyeglasses to do so. As an ecommerce business operator, it's your job to provide an easy, quick, and convenient online shopping experience, regardless of how the customer accesses your site.

Shopify has adopted the unofficial slogan "Sell Everywhere," and it's made that possible with its many tools and resources. However, just because the platform offers many different opportunities to sell products, that does *not* mean you need to (or should) implement all of them. As a startup, it's best to focus on one sales channel or opportunity at a time and then expand to other opportunities later on.

This chapter focuses on the tools available from Shopify and explains how you can use them to establish your company's online presence and sell products in various ways—both via the internet and in the real world.

Establish Your Ecommerce Website Using Shopify

First and foremost, the Shopify platform allows online merchants (i.e., anyone who wants to sell products online) to design, build, publish, and manage a professional-looking ecommerce website using a collection of tools from Shopify, along with a vast selection of optional, third-party plug-ins that can supply all sorts of added functionality to the site.

To get started, simply launch your favorite web browser, visit the Shopify website (https://www.shopify.com/), and click on the Sell pull-down menu option near the top-left corner of the screen (shown in Figure 2.1 below).

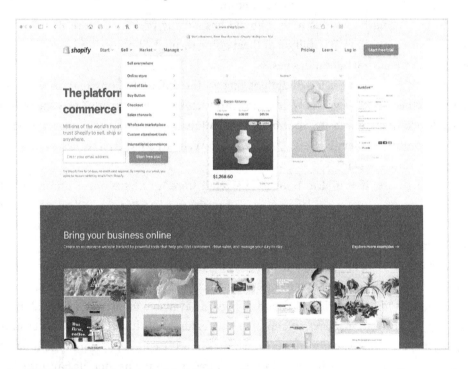

FIGURE 2.1 The tools needed to start creating your ecommerce website are only a few clicks away. From the Shopify website's home page, click on the Sell pull-down menu to get started.

Next, click on the Online Store option near the top of the Sell menu (shown in Figure 2.2 below). Click on the Overview option to start learning about all the tools and resources currently available to help you create, build, publish, and manage your ecommerce website, with absolutely no programming or graphic design skills or experience required.

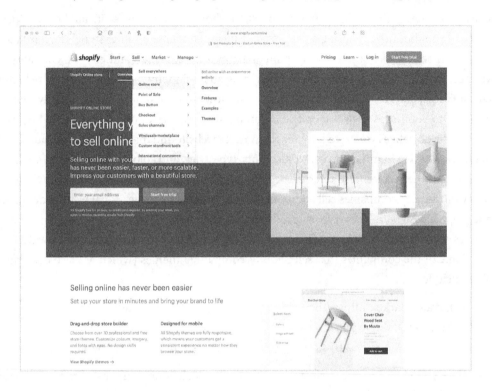

FIGURE 2.2 Shopify offers all the tools needed to create an ecommerce website, starting with a drag-and-drop store builder that gives you access to more than 70 professionally designed, customizable themes.

It's important to understand, however, that while Shopify provides the tools and resources you'll need, it does not provide the assets and content that will allow you to brand and populate your website. It will be your responsibility to write and edit all the text for your website (including the product descriptions), to gather or create the product photography (or video content) your website will showcase, and to brand your website using an original logo and related graphics.

It'll also be your responsibility to come up with and register a unique name and website address (URL) for your business and determine how to differentiate your business and its products from the competition while catering to a niche target audience. And while Shopify's tools will help you market and promote your site, you must still develop, implement, and maintain an ongoing and multifaceted sales, marketing, and promotional plan for your business. (Or, of course, you can hire professionals to help you with any or all of these tasks.)

Shopify's Theme-Based Store Builder

Once you've determined what you want to sell, to whom you want to sell it, and how you plan to brand your business, choosing an appropriate theme should be a rather straightforward task.

The theme you choose will determine the appearance, layout, and core functionality of your ecommerce website, although the great thing about Shopify themes is that they're highly customizable. Start by visiting the directory that showcases the more than 70 Shopify themes available to you (https://www.shopify.com/online/themes). Seek out a theme that'll help you achieve the objectives you have for your ecommerce website and that will appeal to your target audience, keeping in mind you can adjust fonts, typestyles, and color schemes as you see fit.

Beyond the themes (also referred to as website templates) available to you from Shopify, many third-party companies sell additional themes created by professional website designers and graphic designers. These typically sell for between $50 and $100 each, so if one of Shopify's themes doesn't meet your needs, finding a theme that will is only a few extra clicks away.

Some of the companies that sell Shopify-compatible themes (which are also customizable) include:

- Envato Market: https://themeforest.net/category/ecommerce/shopify
- MonsterONE: https://monsterone.com/cms-templates/shopify-themes
- TemplateMonster: https://www.templatemonster.com/shopify-themes.php

Once you've chosen the perfect theme that will match your company's brand, showcase what you're selling, and appeal to your target audience, you can use Shopify's drag-and-drop store builder to populate and customize the theme and start creating your website.

Get the Help You Need When You Need It

As a startup, you can take advantage of the free trial that Shopify offers when you initially set up your account, so you can experiment with the store builder and a few themes while getting acquainted with the Shopify platform and how it operates.

While customizing a Shopify theme is a fairly simple process, if you're not comfortable doing this yourself, you can hire an expert from the Shopify Experts Marketplace (https://experts.shopify.com) to help you.

Shopify Handles Payment Processing

In addition to using the store builder to create your ecommerce website, there's a separate module of Shopify that allows you to set up secure payment options for your customers—

whether or not you already have a credit card merchant account. Using Shopify Payments (https://www.shopify.com/payments), you can set up your website so Shopify handles and processes all your credit and debit card transactions (for an additional fee). The benefits of this, as opposed to setting up your own merchant account with a bank or financial institution, are that you only pay fees when you receive orders, and you are not required to make a long-term commitment.

Down the road, once your online business is successful, it might make sense to negotiate with a bank or financial institution that can provide you with a merchant account that has lower fees, but at least initially, Shopify Payments offers an easy, secure, and risk-free option for processing debit and credit card (Visa, Mastercard, American Express, and Discover) payments.

Shopify Payments also integrates seamlessly with all the popular electronic payment services, including Apple Pay, Google Pay, PayPal, and Facebook Pay, which many online shoppers prefer to use, because it makes them feel safer than having to share their credit or debit card details with an online merchant they have never done business with before.

As of early 2022, when you take advantage of Shopify Payments in conjunction with a Shopify Basic hosting plan that costs $29 a month, expect to pay 2.9 percent of your online sale, plus a 30-cent transaction fee for each online credit card sale, or 2.7 percent of your sale (with no transaction fee) for each in-person credit or debit card sale. These fees should be calculated into your cost of doing business and considered when you're setting your prices. If you upgrade to a different plan, the percentages you pay in fees will vary.

Third-Party Apps Can Expand the Functionality of Your Website

The third component of a Shopify-based ecommerce website, in addition to the features and functionality offered by the Shopify platform and payment options, is the ability to add optional third-party apps (also called plug-ins) to your theme. Each app will add one or more features or functions to your website, and each can often be set up and implemented in a matter of minutes, again with no programming skills required.

The Shopify App Store (https://apps.shopify.com) currently lists more than 6,000 optional third-party apps you can implement into your website. Some are free. Some you pay a one-time fee to use. Others charge a monthly or annual fee or charge a percentage of each sale you generate. As a result, while the optional apps allow you to add a tremendous level of functionality and customizability to your website, you will want to pick and choose which ones you use very carefully.

Incorporating multiple apps into your website also has the potential to slow it down, increase load times, and add on-screen clutter that can distract or confuse your visitors. As you're browsing the Shopify App Store, you'll no doubt discover many flashy bells and whistles that you may think will make your store look awesome.

However, ask yourself whether each app you want to add will provide useful functionality to your website—that is, will it capture the attention of your potential customers in a positive way, improve your conversion rate (transforming visitors into paying customers), or help drive more sales? Will it help you convey your core sales message faster, better showcase what you're selling, or provide additional incentives for your customers to make a purchase?

Anytime an optional app will slow down your website, make it more confusing to navigate, add unnecessary clutter to what your potential customers see, or potentially hamper their ability to find what they need quickly, think very hard before adding that app to your website. Again, always make decisions based on the impact it'll have on your site's visitors and customers, not solely on your own personal preferences.

The Shopify Store Builder Is Chock-Full of Features

Getting back to the Shopify store builder, it offers many benefits beyond the ease of its drag-and-drop interface. All of Shopify's own themes are mobile ecommerce ready, meaning that if a visitor accesses your site from a smartphone or tablet, the site will automatically reformat itself for the smaller screen, providing them with an easy shopping experience.

Plus, if you choose to hire a professional website designer or programmer, you can further customize your theme because you'll have full access to the website's HTML and CSS code. Shopify also gives you the ability to integrate a full-featured blogging platform into your ecommerce website, so you can establish an online community and communicate with your (potential) customers through things like articles, look books, and interactive online discussions.

On the back end, Shopify provides you with a vast collection of tools to help you manage orders and improve your sales conversion rate. You can offer free shipping, set your own shipping rates, or calculate shipping rates for the carriers you choose to work with, such as UPS, DHL, or the U.S. Postal Service (USPS). You can also create a checkout experience in more than 20 languages, have the website automatically calculate taxes based on your location, and give your customers the ability to track their orders.

In addition, Shopify provides comprehensive tools to collect and manage customer profiles and accounts, help with order fulfillment, manage your inventory, integrate seamlessly with dropshipping services, allow you to quickly process refunds, and automatically generate emails. If a potential customer starts placing an order but abandons their cart before checking out, Shopify offers an abandoned checkout recovery tool that will automatically send those potential customers a link to their abandoned order via email and provide whatever additional incentives you set up to encourage them to complete their order.

As an online business operator using the Shopify platform, you can manage every aspect of your website from any internet-connected computer. However, for added convenience, there's also a free Shopify mobile app for merchants.

When it comes to marketing your online business and driving a steady flow of traffic to your website, the Shopify platform offers specialized tools for these tasks, too, including SEO tools, offering your customers special discounts and promo codes, managing and publishing product reviews from your customers, integrating your site with your social media feeds, and the ability to sell gift cards that can be redeemed on your website.

And while you can customize the appearance, design, and layout of your website, you also have full control over how you showcase your products online, with tools that allow you to feature one or more still images or video clips with each product, offer product variations (such as different color or size options), and sell as many separate products as you want from your website, while being able to group together related products as needed.

Meanwhile, available to you on a 24/7 basis are comprehensive analytic reports, so you can see how every aspect of your website is performing in real time. You can opt to view text- and graphics-based reports on products, sales, Google Analytics, traffic, referrals, and so on.

If at any time you have a question or run into a problem, Shopify offers 24/7 technical support by email, telephone, or live chat, plus a comprehensive help center, interactive discussion forums, text and video tutorials, and access to the Shopify Experts Marketplace.

We'll focus more on Shopify's many tools for designing, building, publishing, and managing a professional-looking and branded ecommerce website in Chapter 5, "Creating Your Online Store." For now, understand that this ecommerce turnkey solution most likely offers all the tools, functionality, and resources you'll need at an affordable price.

Shopify Offers Many More Ways to Sell Products Online

Let's explore some of the other ways you can sell your products using tools, services, and resources offered by the Shopify platform that go beyond a traditional ecommerce website.

Point-of-Sale (In-Person) Sales

If you can sell products to customers in person—either on a full-time basis via a brick-and-mortar retail store or just occasionally, Shopify offers the point-of-sale tools and equipment you need to make it an easy process, with minimal fees and no ongoing contracts or commitment.

While selling in person is not the focus of this book, using Shopify's point-of-sale tools for in-person selling is especially useful if you also plan to sell online via a Shopify-based ecommerce website, because everything can be integrated and managed with one back office.

To learn more about the Shopify POS system and other in-person selling tools and resources, and how they can be used on their own or in conjunction with an ecommerce website, visit https://www.shopify.com/pos.

Add a Buy Button to an Existing Website or Blog

If your company already has a website or blog, once you have a Shopify account set up, it's easy to embed individual products or product collections (that are associated with *Buy Buttons*) into your content.

With this feature, someone can be reading an article on your blog, click on a product's Buy Button, and be transported right to a shopping cart to complete their purchase without ever leaving your site.

The ability to create branded product listings (also referred to as *product cards*) that have a Buy Button associated with them is a quick and straightforward process, and you can copy and paste these into your existing content with no programming skills required.

According to the Shopify website (https://www.shopify.com/buy-button), "A Buy Button is a shortcut to the checkout process. With the Shopify Buy Button, merchants can generate an embeddable product card and checkout button that can be added to landing pages or blog posts. This gives shoppers direct purchase access to the merchant's product from whatever web page they see the Buy Button on."

This service is available for as little as $9 per month and allows you to create and implement as many Buy Buttons within your existing content as you wish. You can use it on a stand-alone basis or as an additional sales channel in conjunction with your Shopify-based ecommerce website.

Sell Directly Through Your Social Media Feeds

Many people spend countless hours per day perusing their social media feeds. Once you get to know your target audience and determine their social media habits, you may discover that selling products to them through Facebook, Instagram, TikTok, or some other platform will be a viable option. As with the Buy Button, potential customers can view your products and place an order without ever needing to visit your website.

Using Shopify's tools, you determine what products get showcased, as well as when and where they're promoted on the various social media services. So in addition to using social media as a powerful marketing and promotional tool, you can use it for advertising and direct sales and leverage each social media platform's strengths when appealing to your target audience. Learn more about this feature by visiting https://www.shopify.com/channels.

Take Advantage of Other Online Sales Channels

In some cases, running your own ecommerce website may not be the best approach for selling products online, especially if you're targeting a customer base that's already in the habit of doing their online shopping via Google Shopping, Walmart Marketplace, or eBay.

Shopify can help you set yourself up as an independent seller on any or all of these online marketplaces so you can sell your products directly through them. Thus, instead of creating your own website and working to drive traffic to it, you'll promote your products and then direct customers to your listings on, say, eBay.

If you opt to take this route, keep in mind that you'll need to adhere to the often strict selling and return policies of the platforms you opt to sell through and pay additional fees to list your products. The benefit to you is that you do not need to manage a separate ecommerce website. You just need to create and maintain product listings and then promote your product pages to your customers while taking advantage of the search tools offered by the online marketplaces.

Selling your products via Walmart Marketplace as a certified seller, for example, allows you to tap into the more than 100 million online visitors to Walmart.com who already shop using this service. Once approved, you can list your products for free. You only pay fees when you make a sale.

The process for becoming a seller on Google, Walmart, and eBay, and what you'll need to pay to get started, publish product listings, and process orders is different for each service. One benefit to selling through Google is that your product listings become searchable via the Google search engine, Google Shopping, Google Images, Google Lens, and YouTube (if you publish related video content). Keep in mind, Walmart and eBay offer a selection of other features and tools to also help shoppers find your products. Based on your target audience, what you're selling, and your selling approach, choose services that make the most sense for your business.

To learn more about the direct-selling opportunities available from Shopify via Google, Walmart, and eBay, visit Shopify's website at https://www.shopify.com/channels.

SHOPIFY EXPERT

Alexis Jae
Experienced Shopify Merchant

Before continuing on to Chapter 3, "What Can Be Sold Online," invest a few additional minutes learning from someone who has already accomplished what you hope to achieve—setting up and operating a successful online business using the Shopify platform.

Meet Alexis Jae, whose family has been in the jewelry business for more than 75 years. When she entered her family's occupation, she started her own business by establishing an ecommerce website via Shopify (https://alexisjae.com/), allowing her company to reach a much larger audience with its jewelry staples such as gold hoop earrings and statement necklaces. The company's home page is shown in Figure 2.3 below.

FIGURE 2.3 While the website's design changes periodically, the Alexis Jae site continues to showcase a timeless, sophisticated, and simple design.

Knowing that differentiating her products and establishing a reputable brand was essential, Jae immediately adopted a variety of business practices and policies that set her jewelry apart. Her website allows customers to purchase high-quality, custom-designed gold jewelry (or jewelry that's part of her website's curated collection) for less than half of what they'd pay at a retail store. This includes items that Alexis Jae has chosen to showcase and sell from her online store.

In addition, 25 percent of the company's profits from every sale are donated directly to A Cure in Our Lifetime (https://acureinourlifetime.org), an organization raising funds for breast cancer education and research. Plus, all the 14K and 18K gold used to create the jewelry is 100 percent recycled, while all stones used are natural, untreated, and ethically sourced. Alexis Jae also sells unique pieces designed by its customers.

When you visit Alexis Jae's website (which displays her logo at the top center of the browser window), you'll immediately notice its intentionally simple design and white background, which allows her to put more visual emphasis on the jewelry, as opposed to a site with an overabundance of graphics, animations, and complex menus.

Q: *What made you want to start an ecommerce website?*

My family's been manufacturing fine jewelry for retail stores for generations. After graduating from college, I worked in the finance industry for several years but quit my job to create a website that sells jewelry directly to consumers online.

Originally, I selected Squarespace [https://www.squarespace.com/] as our ecommerce platform because I liked the website design tools it offered, but after launching a website there, it got no traction. When I did more research, I learned about Shopify and discovered it offered much better SEO tools and the ability to link directly with Google. When I switched to Shopify, the migration process was easy. Within a month, I had the new website up and running.

Q: *How did you decide on the appearance of your website?*

I knew the look for the website that I was striving for. I had the whole thing planned out in my head and then on paper. It was then a matter of choosing the right Shopify theme and adapting it to encompass my vision for the site.

Q: *What steps did you take to define your target audience when you first got started?*

When the website was being hosted by Squarespace, we mainly focused on orders from friends and family, as well as their referrals, and whomever else discovered our site.

Once we launched our website on Shopify and began using their analytics tools, we discovered that our jewelry not only resonates with urban women, but also with men from less densely populated areas who are shopping for gifts, and who want beautiful and high-quality jewelry, as opposed to name-brand jewelry. Early on, using the analytics tools provided by Shopify and Google, we learned a lot about who comprised our customer base, and then began focusing on ways to market to this expanded group of people.

Q: *When it came to designing an ecommerce website, what lessons did you learn?*

Instead of adding a whole bunch of optional apps to expand website functionality, which slowed down the site, negatively impacted the user's experience, and had a negative impact on the site's SEO, I wound up hiring a website developer to fine-tune the Shopify theme they selected and add all the customizations and functionality I wanted. This was a more costly option, but I found it was a great investment.

Q: *What are some of the other ways that the Shopify platform has helped your company grow?*

When creating product listings, Shopify directs you to provide specific information in a specific way that benefits your site's SEO. I also took advantage of the integration the platform has for creating and managing blog posts. What I appreciated the most, however, is that without any prior knowledge of how to utilize Google, my site was able to utilize Google Smart campaigns to help promote my business and its products. All I had to do was click on a few buttons and determine how much money I wanted to spend each week on Google ads. The service did everything else and did it very well.

Q: *Initially, what was the biggest misconception you had about selling online?*

I had no idea how difficult it would be to build trust with customers who were shopping online. Our prices are so much lower than well-established jewelry retailers because we are cutting out all the middlemen, but customers don't initially realize how or why we're selling such high-quality jewelry at such low prices.

We hired a copywriter to help us convey our story on our website, to clearly and concisely convey what we're trying to do. Between the design of the overall site and the story we tell through our text and photos, we're now able to tell a compelling story that our visitors relate to and understand. We also try to communicate directly with our customers as much as possible, so they see they're working with a person and not a huge corporation. The copywriter also helps us by writing our marketing emails.

Q: *In addition to hiring a freelance website designer and copywriter, did you hire any additional experts to help you launch the online component of your business?*

Yes. The first person we hired was an SEO specialist who helped us create blog posts. Instead of paying that person upfront, I developed a profit-sharing plan with him. This saved us a lot of money in startup costs and allowed us to benefit from the ability to drive extra traffic to the site. This SEO expert writes three blog posts per week and manages other aspects of the website that impact SEO. We pay him a 20 percent commission on all sales derived from organic searches.

We've also hired a graphic designer, through a friend of a friend, to help us brand our business and fine-tune the appearance of the website. This person designed our logo and helped us choose the appropriate fonts and color scheme used throughout the website. We then hired a social media marketing specialist to help us build up and maintain our Instagram presence, with the goal of driving traffic to the website.

Later, we hired an online marketing agency to utilize the information we acquired from Google to develop and implement our paid online advertising campaigns. The first firm we hired was very inexpensive, but that turned out to be a disaster, so we switched to another online marketing agency that truly understood our vision and goals for the business, as well as the audience we're trying to reach.

While it cost a lot more money upfront, I outsourced everything that I didn't know how to do myself to ensure it would be done correctly. Since we've launched the business, I have invested time to learn a wide range of new skills. For example, I recently completed a class on Google advertising and SEO marketing.

I have found that the website does better when I take on the role of project manager and then hire experts on a freelance basis who have the specialized skills and experience needed to accomplish each task that I am not currently able to do myself. People can be hired in a cost-effective way, and the time and money saved in the long run makes it well worth the expense. There are so many logistics involved with running a successful online business that without additional help, it's very difficult to handle everything and dedicate the time needed to do everything correctly.

Q: *How important is product photography when creating an ecommerce website?*

Having crystal-clear, professional-looking product photography is not just important, it's essential, and it's something we continue to work on, since we're selling high-end jewelry products and it's essential that our product photography nicely showcases each product in a classy way that conveys its beauty and value. We have a professional product photographer on call who photographs every new jewelry piece for the website, as well as a different photographer who creates the lifestyle images used throughout the website.

Q: *Considering all the freelance help you used, how much money would you say you invested to initially get your website designed and published, and to launch the online aspect of your business?*

Keeping in mind that we're selling high-priced jewelry and knew we'd be able to recuperate the investment quickly, I'd calculate that our initial financial investment was about $30,000. Initially, we spent about a month creating the website and developing the brand and then invested a lot more time to tweak it once it launched.

Q: *What's the biggest piece of advice you can share with startup ecommerce business operators?*

Invest the time and money you need upfront to make sure that every aspect of your website functions properly and looks extremely professional. This will help translate visitors to your site into paying customers, because the appearance of your site is your opportunity to make a positive first impression and build up a potential customer's confidence in your company and its products.

Our goal, for example, was to create a website that showcased a high-end brand that was trustworthy. While a company's brand will evolve over time, it's important to use your brand identity right from the start to communicate your value proposition to your potential customers. It's all about building trust with your customers, particularly if you're hoping for repeat business from your customers.

CHAPTER 3

What Can Be Sold Online

Especially because of the COVID-19 pandemic, companies and entrepreneurs have become extremely creative when it comes to developing ways to sell just about anything online. As a rule, if something can be sold from a traditional retail store, it can also be sold online. But (yes, there's a but), if you're an independent online business operator, not every product *should* be sold from your ecommerce *website*.

As you'll discover in this chapter, a lot of consideration should go into the items you choose to sell online. Just about anything that's already being sold by a mass-market super-store like Target, Walmart, or Costco is not a good candidate for your store. The same is true if an item is readily available from retail stores at a local mall or shopping center. You won't be able to compete on price, people won't pay for shipping for items they can easily buy at their local store, and customers will not want to wait a few business days for the item to arrive if they can pick it up immediately at a local store or have Amazon deliver it within a day or two.

What Types of Products Should You Consider Selling Online?

So after taking these items out of the equation, what types of products should you consider selling as a small online business operator?

You'll typically increase your chances of success if you seek out and sell products that are:

- Not readily available at retail stores
- Offered in unusual sizes or colors that retail stores don't typically carry
- Handmade or somehow customized
- Collectible, one of a kind, or antique

- Manufactured only by your company
- Appealing specifically to a niche audience
- Solving a problem or meeting a need
- In demand by consumers but don't have a lot of competition

Once you think you've narrowed down what you want to sell online to one or a handful of related products, you must still consider some additional things before you commit, starting with your inventory costs.

10 Additional Considerations When Choosing What to Sell Online

Ask yourself the following questions to help determine if a product is a viable and potentially profitable option for selling online, especially if you have a limited advertising, marketing, and promotional budget.

1. Can you easily identify the target audience for the product, as well as a secondary target audience the product will appeal to? Will you easily be able to reach this audience (in a cost-effective way) through your ongoing advertising, marketing, and promotional efforts?
2. Will you be able to acquire or manufacture the items cheaply enough that you can still earn a profit after factoring in all your business expenses, operational costs, advertising/marketing costs, and overhead?
3. Will you be able to consistently acquire the inventory you'll need? If one of your suppliers discontinues the product or sells out, can you find more inventory in a timely manner from another source, so you can fulfill your customer orders without delay?
4. Does each product you want to sell solve a problem or fill a need for your customers? Is it in high demand by the niche audience you want to sell to?
5. Will you easily be able to communicate the product's benefits and appeal to your intended customers via a website using text, photos, and/or video?
6. Is the product evergreen, in that it will sell well throughout the year? If the product is seasonal, or will only sell in certain regions, this could make it harder and costlier (and thus less profitable) to promote. Likewise, if the product has a built-in expiration date, you'll have the added challenge of keeping enough on hand to fulfill your orders without getting stuck with inventory that needs to be thrown away once its expiration date approaches.
7. Is the product only popular right now because of a consumer-driven fad or trend? If so, chances are that fad or trend will die in a matter of months, and you could wind up with inventory that's no longer in demand. Keep in mind, it will take weeks or months to get your website fully operational and drive a steady flow of

traffic to the site. By the time you're up and running, the trend could already be coming to an end.

8. Is the product easy and cheap to package and ship, or will you be forced to charge a premium to cover the cost? Keep in mind, customers have grown accustomed to free shipping when making online purchases, so charging for this could be detrimental, unless you're offering something truly unique and that's in demand.

9. Will you encounter too much competition selling your product to the same target audience, forcing you into a price war to stay competitive? Having to undercut your competitors' prices will dramatically reduce or eliminate your ability to earn a profit.

10. Will you easily be able to differentiate your product from the competition and quickly be able to showcase what makes it unique, appealing, or useful to the potential customers visiting your website?

Another thing to consider is whether you'll need to sell multiple variations of each product, in a variety of colors, sizes, or made from different materials. While Shopify can easily accommodate this when creating your product listings, a product with lots of variations means having to maintain a larger inventory and giving your customers decisions to make when placing their order.

Let's say you're selling T-shirts featuring your original designs. Women and men wear different styles of T-shirts, each of which need to come in multiple sizes. You'll probably need to offer each style in adult sizes S, M, L, and XL (you could also expand to XS and XXL or even 3XL or 4XL). You'll have to maintain an even bigger inventory if you offer kids' sizes as well.

Plus, you'll probably want to offer the T-shirt in multiple colors. So for that one T-shirt design, you could easily have 15 to 25 different product options or variations, giving you far more complex logistics to juggle when it comes to manufacturing, maintaining, and storing your inventory. You also need to make sure your sizing options are clear, so customers don't accidentally order the wrong size and then need to return or exchange their purchase, which results in more of a time commitment and greater costs for you.

If you choose to sell 10 different T-shirt designs, you'll be dealing with upward of 100 product variations. Will you have the money and storage space to handle this? (As an alternative, you could have your shirts created using a print-on-demand service once they're ordered and then have them dropshipped to your customers, but this potentially creates another set of challenges, as we discuss below.)

Selling Intangible Products or Subscription-Based Products Is Also an Option

Keep in mind that what you can sell online is not limited to tangible products. Ebooks, audiobooks, enewsletters, video programming, music, NFTs, digital images, software, or any other products that can be purchased and delivered online can be extremely viable options while eliminating your inventory costs.

Meanwhile, if you do choose to sell tangible products, anything that's consumable or that gets routinely used up by the consumer can be sold as an ongoing subscription that you refill on a regular basis. This helps ensure you'll have repeat customers (especially if you provide superior customer service and a high-quality product).

Dropshipping Is an Alternative to Maintaining Inventory

When you see "get rich quick online" schemes promoted, these typically involve setting up a website using a dropshipping business model. You create a website to promote and sell one or more products. However, instead of maintaining an inventory, packaging, and fulfilling your own orders, a third-party company (the dropshipper) does all this on your behalf—eliminating the need to maintain any inventory.

Thus, your startup costs are much lower, there's less of a time commitment, and there's much lower risk. Your job is simply to create a website, promote the product, and get people to buy it from your site. Everything else is up to someone else. Sounds amazing, right?

Even better, Shopify (https://www.shopify.com/dropshipping) makes it easy to set up an ecommerce website and link your online store to one or more dropshipping services they already have a relationship with. When you use one or more of these services, you still want to investigate them, but the Shopify service is already set up to work with them.

For this type of business to work well for you over the long term, however, you must carefully research each dropshipper you plan to work with. Do they maintain a warehouse in the country you're operating from, or will each order be sent from China or another distant country—thus increasing shipping time by something like two weeks to two months? Most customers don't have the patience for this and will shop elsewhere or cancel their order once they learn how long it will take for their goods to arrive from overseas.

When you opt to work with a dropshipper, you become 100 percent dependent on them to maintain enough inventory of your items. If your products wind up being back-ordered and your customers have to wait, it will often result in a canceled order, ill will, or a bad review. It could easily harm the reputation of your brand and your business.

For your business to succeed, the dropshippers you do business with must process orders in a timely manner, make it easy for customers to return or exchange their orders, and package all outgoing orders properly so they don't get damaged in shipping.

You also need to focus on the quality of the products and their packaging. Order several of the products you plan to sell in advance and personally evaluate their quality. You'll find that many products available from overseas dropshippers have incredibly low wholesale prices but poor quality. When you combine this with the fact that a customer may need to wait weeks or months to receive their order, you're pursuing a formula that will result in angry and disappointed customers and a high percentage of returns.

Sure, plenty of extremely successful online businesses use dropshipping. However, if you opt for this route, proceed with caution, do your research, and realize that many aspects of your business will be out of your control when you work with dropshippers, especially if they're overseas.

If you're interested in exploring the dropshipping route using Shopify, there's a 45-minute video seminar on this topic on Shopify's website (https://www.shopify.com/courses/dropship). Use this as a starting point for your research. Finding a niche will require you to do extensive market research and then follow up with some experimentation to see what sells. To help you find products from dropshippers to sell, Shopify links with Oberlo (https://www. oberlo.com/), which is basically a massive directory of dropshippers and the products each one offers.

Keep in mind that you will still need to choose what products to sell; develop and maintain an ecommerce website; advertise, market, and promote the website to drive a steady flow of traffic to it; handle customer service; and be responsible for the day-to-day operation of the business itself with tasks like bookkeeping. There will still be plenty of work and responsibilities for you to deal with, an initial financial investment, and some level of risk you'll need to assume.

Six More Strategies for Achieving Success Using Dropshipping

Once you've selected which products you want to sell and pinpointed which dropshippers you'll use to handle your order processing, consider these six additional strategies to improve your chances for success:

1. *Take all your own product photography.* Do not rely on or use the stock photography provided by the dropshipper, manufacturer, wholesaler, or distributor. Not only will this help you market your products more efficiently to your customers, but it will also help you differentiate your brand and business from the competition.
2. *Write all your own product descriptions.* Again, don't rely on the text provided to you. Make sure each product description is written specifically to appeal to your target audience so that it addresses their unique wants, needs, questions, and potential hesitations when it comes to buying from your site.
3. *Do not make any grandiose or false statements about your products or create false expectations for your potential customers.* Also make sure you don't infringe on anyone else's copyrights or trademarks. Even if it's not required by law, make sure you use terms like *guaranteed, ethically sourced, handmade, cruelty-free, biodegradable, fair trade, made from [insert number] percent recycled [insert*

material], eco-friendly, or *all-natural* appropriately and accurately (even if your dropshipper or competition uses phrases that you know are embellished or outright lies).

4. *Consider comparing, feature for feature, the products you sell with those of your competition.* Highlight what sets your products and company apart and show why potential customers should buy from you. You should be 100 percent confident in your product's quality and know everything there is to know about it.

5. *Be upfront and honest about shipping time, especially if your products will be shipped from abroad and take weeks (or months) to arrive at the customer's door.* Again, create realistic expectations.

6. *Line up at least one or two backup suppliers you can rely on if your primary dropshipper discontinues the products you're selling, runs out of inventory, or suddenly goes out of business.* Failing to have a backup plan in place could result in your company having to refund outstanding orders or needing to shut down altogether.

Define Your Product Offerings

Based on your skill set and interests, chances are you already have a pretty good idea about what you want to sell online via your ecommerce website. Now it's time to define your initial product offerings.

What are the main items you plan to sell, and what colors, designs, sizes, and other options will you offer to your customers? Once you figure this out, start brainstorming related products you could offer to your niche target audience. For example, if you plan to sell leather dress shoes crafted in Italy, consider expanding your offerings to include dress socks and various accessories for storing and polishing the shoes.

Based on the size, design, and color options you plan to offer for each product, think about what your inventory requirements will be and how you'll showcase and describe each option as part of a product listing on your website. (Fortunately, the Shopify store builder makes it easy to add these options to each product listing as you create them.)

Use the worksheet in Figure 3.1 on page 33 to help define what products you'll initially offer in your ecommerce store and what related products you might want to add in the future. Each item will be given its own product listing, but within that listing and during the checkout process, you can offer multiple options to the customer (e.g., allowing them to choose size, color, material, or customization).

Inventory Considerations

Your inventory can come from many different sources. It could be made up of products you purchase from a manufacturer, wholesalers, or distributors in bulk. Or it could include

Product Name	Product Description	Size Options to Be Offered	Color Options to Be Offered	Customizations or Other Customer-Selectable Options to Be Offered	Will the Product Be Offered Immediately or in the Future?

FIGURE 3.1 Product Worksheet: Use this worksheet to help define what products you'll initially offer in your ecommerce store and what related products you might want to add in the future.

products that you designed and had custom-manufactured, or products you handcrafted yourself in-house, using materials you purchased in bulk.

No matter where you acquire your inventory, one of your ongoing challenges will be to ensure you always have enough stock on hand to quickly fill and ship your orders. Depending on what you'll be selling, you may need to be prepared for a sudden influx of sales during a holiday season, in conjunction with a new advertising campaign, or after your company or products are featured in a blog, podcast, or magazine.

Learning to accurately determine how much inventory you need to keep on hand and how often you must replenish it is a skill you'll acquire over time, but it's also a calculation you can't afford to get wrong when a customer places an order on your website and expects it to be delivered within a few days.

In situations where you're customizing a product or making it from scratch as each order comes in, you must make it clear on your website how long they will need to wait so you can set realistic expectations. An online business called Little Felted Friends (https://littlefeltedfriends.com) sells one-of-a-kind, handcrafted sculptures of people's pets made out of wool felt. This company only accepts orders via its website on the first day of the month, starting at 10 a.m. EST, and it is very clear about the fact that new orders will take up to four months to ship.

Avoid the Most Common Inventory-Related Mistake

If your ecommerce business will rely on manufacturers, suppliers, wholesalers, or distributors to provide your inventory or the materials you need to create your inventory, you must always have a backup plan to source the products or materials you need quickly if a problem arises with your primary suppliers.

One of the worst mistakes ecommerce business operators can make is spending weeks or months to create an incredible website and investing hundreds or thousands of dollars on a marketing campaign to drive traffic to their site and acquire orders, only to discover that when the time comes to replenish their inventory, it will take weeks or months to get enough stock to fill their outstanding orders. As a result, customers cancel their orders and the company develops a poor reputation.

Where to Store Your Inventory

Because many startup ecommerce businesses are homebased, you'll need to set aside space in your home to safely store your inventory, ideally in a temperature-controlled area. If your basement, garage, or attic is damp, prone to floods, or a place where mold or mildew grows quickly, do not store your inventory there, as the risk of its being damaged or destroyed is too high.

Again, depending on what you'll be selling and the level of inventory you'll need to maintain, it might make sense for you to use an outside storage facility. While this will free up space within your home, it'll also be an added monthly expense and require you to drive there whenever you need more inventory. So you'll need to decide whether the added hassle and expense are worth it.

Your Ecommerce Business Needs Business Insurance

If you're operating your business from your home, your homeowners or renters insurance does *not* cover your company's inventory, business equipment, or other assets if your home is robbed or damaged by a flood or fire. Thus you'll need to buy adequate small business insurance in addition to your regular homeowners or renters insurance.

The Small Business Administration's (SBA) website offers comprehensive information about which of the six common types of business insurance you'll need and can help you calculate the appropriate level of coverage required for your business to meet legal requirements. You can then contact local licensed insurance brokers or shop for insurance online. As your business grows, you'll want to reassess your insurance needs every year.

Depending on where you're based, some of the reputable insurance companies you might want to research include:

- *Liberty Mutual Insurance*: https://business.libertymutual.com/small-business-dashboard
- *Nationwide*: https://www.nationwide.com/business
- *Progressive*: https://www.progressive.com/insurance/#business
- *State Farm*: https://www.statefarm.com
- *The Hartford*: https://www.thehartford.com/business-insurance
- *Travelers*: https://www.travelers.com/business-insurance

Be Sure to Research Your Competition

Coming up with what you believe are the ideal products to sell and then using the Shopify platform to create the perfect website to sell those items to your target audience are all necessary steps to achieve success. However, right from the start, you also need to consider who your competition is and develop a plan to deal with them.

Start by researching exactly who they are. Once you identify each of your competitors, become one of their customers and purchase the products that will compete directly with what you plan to sell. As you do this, pay careful attention to every aspect of the experience.

Ask yourself these 15 questions about each competitor:

1. Is their website professional looking and well-designed?
2. How reputable is the competitor? Are their ratings and reviews prominently displayed?
3. Is their website easy to navigate?
4. Is their shopping cart experience well-implemented?
5. Are their product descriptions accurate, detailed, informative, concise, and easy to understand?
6. How well does the website tell the company's story?
7. How good is the customer service? Are the company's operators easily accessible, friendly, and helpful?
8. What payment options do they offer?
9. Does the website have any especially good features, functions, or bells and whistles? Are there any that you believe are confusing, distracting, or unnecessary?
10. Will you be able to compete with the competitor's pricing?
11. Do they offer free shipping or special discounts to first-time or repeat customers?
12. What aspects of the website particularly appeal to their target audience?

13. How do they differentiate themselves from their competition?

14. What are the problems or drawbacks you see with the competitor's website?

15. How do you think you will do things better than your competition?

As you evaluate your competitors, pay particular attention to their brand and pricing. Is the company focusing on selling its products at the lowest price possible and competing mainly on that, or has it adopted a premium-pricing model by creating a more upscale shopping experience for its customers?

In addition to researching your online-based competition, determine if you have competition from retailers or sellers operating in the real world and evaluate how each might impact the success of your business. Once you determine how much competition you'll have from sellers in the real world and online, you'll need to figure out a way to compete with them so that your business will appeal to your target customers, take over some of the overall market share, and earn a healthy profit.

Keep in mind that the more popular your products become, and the more success you experience, the harder your competitors will work to steal your customers. Make it a habit to reassess your competition at least once per month, and then tweak your business model, website, and marketing accordingly so you can stay one step ahead of them.

When new visitors come to your website, among the questions on their minds will be:

- "Where can I find a similar product for less money?"
- "How is this product better than the competition?"
- "Is this company more reputable than their competition?"
- "Does this website offer a faster, easier, and more convenient shopping experience than the competition?"
- "If I have a problem with the product, will the seller help me resolve the problem, process an exchange quickly, or provide a refund?"
- "This website is selling the product I want for more money than I've seen it elsewhere. Why? Is paying a premium price worth it to do business with this particular company?"

The shopping experience your website offers should address these questions quickly and put the customer's mind at ease while making it clear that your business and its products are better than the competition. The overall quality, design, and appearance of your website; the clarity of your product descriptions; the visual appeal of your product images; and the story your website tells about your company can all help you establish yourself as a reputable seller.

Tips for Setting Your Prices and Developing a Premium Brand

When it comes to setting fair prices for your products, there's no one formula that works for every business and every product. First, however, you must calculate all your overhead business expenses: inventory costs, shipping costs, credit/debit card payment processing fees, Shopify fees, advertising and marketing costs, salary-related expenses, and desired profit margin. Only then can you accurately determine the lowest price you can sell each product for and still earn a profit from each sale. We'll talk more about how to do this below.

One of the worst mistakes you can make as an ecommerce business operator, especially as a startup, is competing exclusively on price. This may work for the short term, but it's often not sustainable, and before long you'll start to lose money on each sale.

A more strategic approach is to sell your products at a price you can justify by providing a top-notch, easy, and enjoyable shopping experience for your customers. An even better approach is to establish your products and company as a premium brand and then charge higher prices than your competition. If you take this approach, a stellar reputation is essential, and you must be able to showcase exactly why a customer should pay more to buy from your company.

You can charge premium prices by offering a superior shopping experience, better customer service, higher-quality products, better product packaging, and other ways to increase the perceived value of your wares. Customers, especially affluent and well-educated ones, are willing to pay more for a product if you can create a higher perceived value and offer them value-added benefits or perks. Once you've determined what you plan to sell and to whom you plan to sell it, brainstorm ways you can establish yourself as a premium seller offering superior products your customers will pay more money for.

Even if you're selling to a lower- to middle-income target audience, if you can make customers perceive your products as being better and more valuable than the competition, you'll have an easier time charging a high price for them. What you never want to do is get into a price war with your competition and try to constantly undercut your competitors. Eventually, this will drive your profits way down and make your business model unsustainable.

How to Calculate Your Product's Retail Price

Before you can determine a retail price for each product you'll be selling, you need to determine your tool/equipment costs, materials/supply costs, product packaging costs, shipping costs, marketing/advertising/promotional costs, one-time and ongoing business startup costs, and overhead (operations) costs. This includes how much you want to be paid for your time and the profit you'd like to earn from each sale.

Knowing this will help you set the wholesale (if applicable) and retail prices for whatever you'll be selling. The widely accepted formula for setting prices can be calculated by following these steps:

1. Calculate the cost of your materials/supplies per item. For this example, let's say your materials/supplies cost is $10 per item. You'll also need to calculate other costs

related to each item, like packaging costs, and shipping costs that you might want to pass onto the customer. Add this to your total cost for a product.

2. Amortize the fixed tool costs and overhead costs for your business and calculate what percentage needs to be covered per item you will be selling. Let's say this comes out to $15 per item. (Your bookkeeper or accountant can help you come up with a list of these costs, which will be specific to your business.)

3. If you'll be customizing, crafting, or manufacturing your products in-house, figure out how long it'll take you to make each item. Next, calculate the cost of your time, based on the hourly wage you set for yourself. So if each item takes you two hours and you opt to pay yourself $10 per hour, the cost of your time per item is $20. If you're not creating your own products, add an hourly wage for your time that covers the work you do.

4. How much profit per item do you want/need to earn to keep your business afloat and stay happy? This markup should be realistic and acceptable by your customers. Let's go with $5 per item for this exercise.

Add together the cost per item for steps one through four. For this example, you'd add $10 + $15 + $20 + $5, which comes out to $50. This is your cost to create or acquire the item for your inventory. To calculate your wholesale price per item, double your cost. Thus, for this product, the wholesale price would be $100.

To calculate the retail price (what you will charge customers on your website), double the wholesale price—so the price you'd charge for this item online would be $200. Otherwise, list the shipping and handling options and related fees separately and have Shopify add this to your customer's subtotal during the checkout process. Your website can also be set up to calculate and charge sales tax, if applicable. Sales tax does not need to be built into the retail price of your items.

Depending on what you're selling, consumer demand, your competitors' pricing, and other related factors, you may need to adjust your prices to stay competitive by reducing your manufacturing/inventory costs, spending less on advertising, or lowering your hourly wage a bit.

However, if you're offering something unique, rare, or that requires exceptional skill or talent to produce, you'll likely be able to charge a premium. How you promote your brand and create perceived value will also be a major factor in determining what customers will be willing to pay for your products.

Your goal is to price your products fairly and competitively and in a way that allows you to generate a reasonable profit. Of course, you must also be able to negotiate the lowest prices possible from your manufacturers, suppliers, distributors, and wholesalers, so you can keep your product creation and/or inventory prices as low as possible.

Of course, you can set any price you want for the items you're selling. However, if you want customers to buy them, they need to believe your products are worth the prices you're charging. Ask yourself why a buyer should purchase your products instead of the competition's.

Perhaps the answer is that your products are made from better materials and their overall quality is much higher. Maybe your products showcase more intricate and complex craftsmanship, or they offer additional features or functions that the competition's products do not.

Whatever is unique about each of your products must be detailed clearly in your product descriptions and, if possible, emphasized in your photographs. Never assume that your customers will automatically see what's special about your products or that the differentiating factors between your products and the competition's are obvious. Promote it in your online store, your product listings and photography, your advertising and marketing, and your company's story.

When showcasing individual products in your online store, group together similar or related products and, when appropriate, offer special bundles of your products at a discounted price. This will make it easier for your customers to find what they're looking for and potentially purchase more than they originally planned.

Identify Your Target Audience

Throughout this book and in many of its featured interviews, you'll repeatedly read how important it is to target your ecommerce business to a niche target audience and do everything within your power to cater to their unique wants, needs, and expectations.

But you first need to understand what a niche audience or target audience is. Basically, it's a specific group of people you can identify who want or need your product, based on a variety of demographic and/or geographic criteria. Let's say that your company's target audience is college-educated women between the ages of 18 and 34, who earn more than $50,000 per year, live in a city, juggle a full-time job with parenting, and spend time on Instagram. Because you'll be selling to people online, your target audience must also be internet-savvy and comfortable shopping on their computer or mobile device.

The more precisely you can describe your target audience, the easier it'll be to create an ecommerce website that caters to them and then implement sales, marketing, and promotional campaigns that reach this audience in the most cost-effective ways. You'll be in a better position to address their needs and wants and explain how what you're selling will solve a problem they have or somehow improve their life. At the same time, you can help them overcome any hesitation they may have about buying from your website.

In fact, once you determine the target audience for your company and products, just about every decision you'll need to make about operating your business—designing your website, setting your prices, marketing your products, driving traffic to your website, and converting website visitors into buyers—should be based on everything you know about them.

Your company's niche target audience description can consist of as many demographic and/or geographic identifiers as necessary, and should include at least several of the following:

- Age
- Buying/shopping habits
- Club or association memberships
- Computer usage
- Employment status
- Family composition
- Gender
- Geographic location
- Hobbies
- Income
- Level of education
- Level of technical knowledge
- Marital status
- Mobile device usage
- Occupation
- Physical attributes (including height and/or weight)
- Political affiliation
- Religion
- Residence type (house, apartment, condo, etc.)
- Sexual orientation
- Social media habits
- Spending habits
- Where they work and the company they work for
- Whether they have one or more credit or debit cards
- Willingness to shop online

After clearly defining the primary target audience for your business, consider additional secondary audiences your products will likely appeal to. Initially, you'll probably want to focus on your primary target audience, but later, when it comes to expanding your business and choosing additional products to offer, you may want to begin catering to other target audiences as well.

Also, if your products cater to people experiencing a major event in their life (such as an engagement, marriage, divorce, birth of a child, job promotion, bar or bat mitzvah, sweet 16, graduation, or retirement), this too should be included in the detailed description of your company's target audience.

Compose Attention-Grabbing and Informative Product Descriptions

When it comes to creating individual product listings for your ecommerce website, the listing's headline, text, and keywords associated with it should all be written in a way that's easy to understand, concise, and relatable to your target audience.

In just a few sentences, your product description needs to make it clear why someone from your target audience needs your product, why they should want it, how it will solve a problem they have, how it will save them time or money, and how using it will somehow improve the overall quality of their life.

At the same time, your product description needs to highlight the key features and functions of the product, its quality, what sets it apart from the competition, and any other key pieces of information about the product that your target audience wants or needs to know.

Your product descriptions cannot contain any spelling or grammatical mistakes and should only use language that your target audience will understand, relate to, and respond favorably to. Each description also needs to be 100 percent truthful, create realistic expectations about the product, and include at least one or two precisely worded calls to action that will ideally make the potential customer immediately click or tap on the Buy Button. That's a tall order.

As you can see, composing effective product descriptions is an art form unto itself, and a skill that'll take time to master. If you don't consider yourself a prolific and talented writer and marketer, consider hiring an experienced freelance writer who specializes in product listings and sales content for ecommerce websites. (How and where to find these people is covered in Chapter 7, "Sources of Help.")

Creating Professional-Quality Product Photos Is Essential

Choosing the right products to sell and then writing attention-grabbing product descriptions are both extremely important. However, equally important is being able to showcase crystal-clear, well-lit, highly detailed, and professional-looking photographs of those products.

If a customer visits a retail store, they can see, touch, try out, smell, and even sometimes taste a product before purchasing it. But when they shop online, they're limited to learning about the product through the description, photographs (or videos), ratings and reviews, and any additional research they do.

For this reason, every product for sale on your website should be accompanied by several product photos. As you'll learn in Chapter 5, "Creating Your Online Store," the photos should be taken against a simple background, be well-lit, and allow customers to see the product and its features and functions from a variety of different angles. Thus, you'll probably want to include between three and five images with each product listing.

In addition to the product images, you'll also likely want to include several lifestyle photos with each product listing. These are images that show your product being used in the real world. If you're selling handmade gold and diamond earrings, your lifestyle images might show a model wearing the earrings while dressed in formal, work, and casual outfits.

Rounding out your photography needs for your website will be branding photography. These images will help the potential customer get to know your brand and help convey your company's unique story. Branding photos might include behind-the-scenes images of your workshop, where you handcraft or manufacture your products.

Meanwhile, if you can afford it, including at least one short video that showcases and demonstrates the product will go a long way toward helping you sell it to potential customers. If you opt to use video, each clip must be produced with the highest quality possible (with perfect lighting and sound).

One of the biggest mistakes startup ecommerce website operators make is cutting corners when it comes to photography. They either use generic stock images (which appear on numerous websites, including the competition), or they take their own shots using amateur-level equipment and no experience whatsoever.

The result is a collection of images with poor lighting and shadows that do not show details and are visually unappealing. This conveys a negative message to website visitors and damages your company's credibility and product value.

Because the quality of the photography (or videos) is so important, and since each image or video clip needs to visually appeal and cater to your target audience, it often makes sense to hire a professional freelance photographer or videographer to create and edit this content for you. How and where to find these people is covered in Chapter 7, "Sources of Help."

The key takeaway for now is that every image and graphic on your website should appeal to your target audience, convey important information about your company and its products, and help potential customers believe your company is a high-quality and reputable brand.

Bob Herman
Cofounder of Luv To Laugh

Luv To Laugh (https://luvtolaugh.com) is a Shopify-based ecommerce website that sells graphic designs created by Bob Herman's brother Scott, which are imprinted on T-shirts and other apparel. Most of the company's orders are created and fulfilled by print-on-demand services.

Herman is an engineer and the cofounder of IT Tropolis (https://ittropolis.com) by trade, which offers managed IT services to businesses. While this continues to be his full-time job, Luv To Laugh represents a part-time side business cofounded by Herman and Scott. While his brother handles the creative side of the business, Herman handles all technical aspects, including the ongoing operation of Luv To Laugh's website (shown in Figure 3.2 below).

FIGURE 3.2 The Luv To Laugh website sells original artwork on apparel that's created using print-on-demand services.

In this interview, you'll learn more about Herman's experience creating and managing their online business using Shopify.

Q: *How did the concept for Luv To Laugh evolve into an ecommerce website?*

My brother and I wanted to create something to honor the memory of our grandmother, who we called Bubby. She always loved to laugh, and the graphic designs featured on our apparel are based on her adventures. Once we determined what our goals would be for the company, we conducted research to learn about the ecommerce platforms that could best meet our needs.

We wound up choosing Shopify because we felt that the admin console for managing the site was the most intuitive and the third-party apps that can be incorporated into the site to add functionality are expansive. The cost to operate an ecommerce business using Shopify is also very affordable, especially considering that website hosting is included. By providing us with the technological tools needed to easily create and manage the website, this allowed us to focus more on creating the products we wanted to launch.

Q: *Part of your company's brand and philosophy includes supporting the charity Feed the Hungry (https://www.feedthehungry.org/), and you donate 5 percent of your net profits to this organization. What made you decide to do this?*

There are many charities out there that support causes around feeding people who are hungry. As we were first coming up with ideas for Luv To Laugh, we knew that we wanted to support some type of charity. We chose a charity that we believed was important to the world and that our bubby would also have supported and believed in. Ultimately, as we learned about Feed the Hungry, we decided that this was a great cause that we wanted to support.

Q: *Why did you decide to use a print-on-demand service to imprint your products?*

We actually work with several different print-on-demand services, and we love the fact that they integrate seamlessly with Shopify. Choosing to use a print-on-demand service to create our products and fulfill our orders was purely a financial decision. We simply could not afford to initially create and maintain an inventory. As we grow, we plan to begin having our products manufactured in bulk and carrying our own inventory, because ultimately this would allow us to earn higher profits from each sale.

Q: *What was the biggest misconception you initially had about starting an ecommerce business?*

We had inaccurate expectations for sales volume. When we were telling our friends and family about the business idea, everyone was incredibly supportive, so we thought that quickly getting a bunch of orders would be easy because everyone would just love the idea once they discovered our website. We did not have the initial marketing budget to generate the traffic and sales we initially expected.

Q: *What would you say are some of the key skills someone needs to create and manage a successful ecommerce business?*

While much of the Shopify platform relies on an intuitive user interface, there's still an overall learning curve when it comes to understanding how ecommerce, as well as online sales and marketing, actually works. People need to understand the Shopify platform and learn how to use it before they launch their business on the platform. It's important to understand how everything works and understand things like shipping rates and how the various online ad platforms work. Most of our paid advertising is done through social media and email marketing, and it's important to learn how to do this properly, or you can easily wind up misspending your money.

Q: *From the time you and your brother came up with the idea for Luv To Laugh to the time your website was launched, how long did the process take?*

We spent about six months putting everything together, creating the designs for our products, and developing a business plan we were comfortable with. Initially, we chose to launch the business with a specific number of designs, with the plan to continuously launch new designs. We did not want to provide customers with too many choices initially, so the goal was to create four distinct collections, and then have about 10 different products in each collection.

Q: *How did the brand for your business evolve?*

We wanted to establish our brand first, before ever launching the website. We came up with the business name and Luv To Laugh brand knowing we wanted something that could have a broad focus and that would allow us to expand in the future. A name like Bubby's Adventures would have been too narrow a focus. After brainstorming the name, we didn't finalize it till we knew we could get the domain name and had a logo that could be trademarked. The company name and brand project exactly the message we want to convey.

I believe it's important to establish a brand for a company at the very beginning, and the brand should represent something you're very passionate about that has a definable and reachable target audience—not too broad or too niche.

Q: *What type of research did you do about the competition you'd encounter?*

We thought a lot about the competition as we were developing the concept for and focus of the business. When creating our products, we were very careful not to create something that would have to compete directly in the already-crowded marketplace for low-priced T-shirts with imprinted funny sayings. Our focus was on creating unique artwork, for which we hoped people would be willing to pay a premium.

It's very tricky coming up with a price for your products that allows you to earn a profit yet stay in line with the competition. A lot depends on what you're selling, who you're selling to, and the perceived value you can create for your products. Creating a premium brand that sells higher-quality products and then differentiating your products from the competition are strategies that allow a company like ours to charge higher prices.

Q: *On your website, what are some of the strategies you use to quickly establish your company as a premium-priced brand?*

We promote that our products are all custom-made using premium-quality materials, inks, and fabrics, and that we use a higher-quality printing process than most of our competitors. Our printing process does not peel or fade over time. We use our product descriptions to communicate this information to the prospective buyer.

When creating product titles and descriptions, it's important to provide a lot of information in a very concise manner. For example, you want to keep your product titles to 65 characters in length or shorter, especially if you're integrating your website with advertising platforms. You also want to incorporate SEO-appropriate keywords and phrases into your product titles and descriptions. Of course, you absolutely need to proofread everything before publishing it.

Q: *Once you decided to use the Shopify platform, how did you choose the theme for your website?*

We had a vision in mind for what we wanted the website to look like. We ultimately chose a free theme called Debut, but now that the website is established, we're looking at changing the theme. Applying a theme and previewing what your entire site will look like is very easy with Shopify.

Choosing the right theme for your business is important. Some themes are only appropriate for specific types of businesses. Regardless of which theme you choose, make sure you understand how to customize it. Otherwise, you need to be willing to hire someone to help you with the customization process.

Q: *Between you and your brother, you have professional and creative skills that are very conducive to creating and managing an ecommerce business. As you were getting started, did you need to hire any experts to help you accomplish specific tasks?*

We have hired a professional photographer on a freelance basis to help us with product photography, although several print-on-demand services we work with provide us with high-quality mock-ups of the products that can be used online. Keep in mind, the photographer you hire should be able and willing to edit the photos as needed, so they can be incorporated directly onto your website in the appropriate file format and size.

Q: *You mentioned that you use social media as an advertising and marketing tool. Which social media services have proved most successful for you?*

For us, Facebook has worked well. We have a Facebook page for the company, and we use Facebook advertising as well. Right from Day One, get all your friends and family involved with your company's social media presence, and get those people to invite their online friends to your company's Facebook page. I have found that paid Facebook advertising works well for us. Shopify makes it easy to use Facebook advertising in an effective and affordable way.

When it comes to online advertising, always start off small and perform tests before investing lots of money. Also try experimenting with different target audiences for your ads. With Facebook, you can get very granular in how you target people. Doing this will allow you to see how your products resonate with various niche audiences. One thing I have learned firsthand is that it's going to take more online advertising dollars than you think to get your brand out there, build momentum, and drive a steady flow of traffic to your site.

One marketing strategy we're currently looking at is how we can attract social media influencers to help promote our products through paid endorsements. I believe this is something that could work well for us, but it has not yet been within our marketing budget. Cameo [https://www.cameo.com/] is a great service for finding affordable B-list celebrities to record short promotional videos for your brand that can be featured on your website and on social media, for example.

The approach you take with your product listings, photography, and videography will depend on what you're selling, who you're selling to, and what story you want to communicate with the people who visit your website.

You Have Many More Steps to Complete Before Launching Your Business

Before you can start selling anything online, you need to establish your company as a legal business entity. Even if you're starting a part-time business from home with the goal of supplementing your income, as soon as you publish your website and start selling anything online, you're operating a legitimate business. You're thus responsible for paying taxes on your income and setting up your business in a way that meets local, state, and federal requirements.

The focus of Chapter 4, "Establishing Your Business," is how to organize your business as a legal entity and handle all the tasks associated with setting up a new business from scratch, including choosing a business name and domain name, developing your brand, and writing a business plan.

Establishing Your Business

Before you launch and start promoting your ecommerce website, you need to complete a number of steps: naming your business, developing your brand, setting up your company as a legal business entity, gathering startup capital, putting together an operating budget, setting up a bookkeeping system, opening a business bank account, acquiring business insurance, setting up your home office (or a traditional office), and composing a well-thought-out business plan.

Every business operator needs to complete these steps when they start a new business, and you'll need to do them as well if you want your business to have a strong foundation.

Depending on your knowledge base and previous business experience, during this startup process it might make sense to consult with a lawyer, an accountant, an insurance broker, and a local banker—each of whom can provide guidance and help you avoid potentially costly mistakes.

According to the SBA (https://www.sba.gov/business-guide/10-steps-start-your-business), the 10 core steps of establishing a startup business (including an ecommerce business) are:

1. Conducting market research
2. Composing a business plan
3. Funding the business
4. Choosing a location for your business
5. Choosing an appropriate legal structure
6. Selecting a business name
7. Registering the business
8. Obtaining state and federal tax ID numbers

9. Applying for licenses and permits (if applicable)

10. Opening a business bank account

Each one of these core steps might require you to complete a handful of additional tasks.

Get the Business Guidance You Need, Right from the Start

The best way to find referrals for the expert help you'll likely need is through word-of-mouth from people you already know and trust. However, you can find help by using many other resources, including these:

- *Freelancer*: https://www.freelancer.com/info/how-it-works
- *LinkedIn Services Marketplace*: https://www.linkedin.com/services
- *Shopify Experts*: https://experts.shopify.com
- *Upwork*: https://www.upwork.com/

Another useful resource is called SCORE, or the Service Corps of Retired Executives (https://www.score.org/). It's a nonprofit organization and the nation's largest network of volunteer expert business mentors. Their mission is to help small businesses get off the ground, grow, and achieve their goals. Since 1964, SCORE has provided education and mentorship to more than 11 million entrepreneurs.

As well as pairing up startup and small businesses with mentors, the organization's website offers free resources, including the Startup Roadmap (https://www.score.org/startup-roadmap), a step-by-step guide for starting a business, and the SCORE Business Learning Center (https://www.score.org/biz-learning-center), which offers free online courses on hundreds of topics useful to anyone starting or operating a small business or startup.

The SBA (https://www.sba.gov/) also offers free educational resources and referrals to entrepreneurs and small business operators (especially those in the startup phase). It has online courses that'll help you plan, launch, manage, market, and grow your business and provides free tools you might need to acquire a business loan. One of the best things about the SBA is that the organization can provide the personalized guidance you need, typically for free.

The U.S. Business Association of Ecommerce (https://usbaec.com) has a library of online learning tools and resources available to its members; fees start at $19.97 per month for small business operators. Even for nonmembers, this organization offers an informative blog (https://usbaec.com/red/blogs) with hundreds of articles and tutorials of interest to ecommerce website operators.

When it comes to setting up your business as a legal business entity (a DBA/sole proprietorship, partnership, LLC, or corporation), obtaining a state or federal tax ID number, filing for a copyright or trademark, or handling a variety of other tasks that many people find confusing or complicated, a less expensive route than hiring a lawyer is to use the services of a company like LegalZoom (https://www.legalzoom.com/). Instead of charging by the hour, LegalZoom has a flat fee for each task it handles (plus local, state, or federal filing fees).

Start by Naming Your Business

Every business needs a name. The name you choose should be descriptive, unique, easy to remember, easy to spell, and relatable to your target audience—and you need to make sure it doesn't violate another organization's copyrights or trademarks. Coming up with the perfect name for your business is the first step in creating an overall brand.

When choosing a name, make sure it's scalable. Let's say right now you want to sell widgets, so you choose the name John's Widget Company. But if in a few years you decide to expand to other products, "John's Widget Company" will no longer be a good match for your business. Also avoid choosing a name based on current trends. Fads come and go, but your business name should be timeless.

Start by coming up with at least a dozen words that somehow describe your business and its primary goals. You can then use this word list as inspiration for a company name. Try combining words to create a name that's unique yet descriptive, and helps tell your company's story. During your brainstorming process, also consider abbreviations. Some of the best-known company names, like 3M, AT&T, BMW, CVS, GEICO, IBM, and UPS, are abbreviations.

To help you create a name for your business, Shopify offers a free business name generator (https://www.shopify.com/tools/business-name-generator). The Wix website design service also offers a free business name generation tool (https://bit.ly/3y9qk0W).

Come up with a list of at least 10 to 20 potential company names you like, and then do some market research to determine how that company name resonates with your target audience. You should also research how your proposed name compares with your competition and check that no other company has registered the name as a copyright or trademark. You can do this at the websites for the U.S. Copyright Office (https://www.copyright.gov/public-records/) and U.S. Patent and Trademark Office (https://www.uspto.gov/trademarks/search). Next visit any domain name registrar, such as GoDaddy (https://www.godaddy.com/), and make sure the URL for that name is available with the .com extension. As soon as you finalize your company name, register that domain name, even if you haven't yet started work on the website.

You have the option of using more than 1,500 domain name extensions in addition to .com, including .biz, .info, .store, .club, .online, .tech, and .vip. While you may want to register your company's domain name using one or more of these extensions as well (for an additional annual fee), it's essential to own the .com version, because that's what most people will automatically type in when looking for your company. (To learn more about domain name extensions and how you can use them for marketing purposes, visit https://www.godaddy.com/domains/gtld-domain-names.)

The YourCompanyName.com URL you register will serve as the primary way visitors access your ecommerce website via their web browser. When you use Shopify to create your website, Shopify will assign a long URL to your site. However, you can use your domain name registrar's forwarding tool or use Shopify's tools to automatically connect your domain name to your Shopify website.

Create a Professional Company Logo

After coming up with the perfect name for your company, you'll need a unique logo that represents the company visually. Unless you have previous graphic design and visual marketing skills and experience, invest a few hundred dollars to hire a professional graphic designer to create both color and black-and-white versions of your company logo.

Your logo will be one of the first things that a visitor to your website sees, so it's important that it makes a positive impression and resonates well with your target audience. In addition to appearing throughout your website, the same logo should be displayed on your product packaging, your outgoing emails, your social media content, and all printed materials related to your business (letterhead, business cards, product brochures, shipping labels, invoices, etc.).

Your logo should be simple, visually appealing, and easy to recognize and remember. While a logo can simply consist of your company name in a specific color and font, it might also include some type of graphic or shape. Keeping your target audience in mind, work with your graphic designer to create a logo that best fits your company's brand.

For additional tips on how to create a professional logo, read the articles and blog posts on these websites:

- *99designs*: "How to Design a Logo: The Ultimate Guide," https://99designs.com/blog/logo-branding/how-to-design-logo
- *Canva*: "Free Logo Maker," https://www.canva.com/create/logos/
- *Design Shack*: "10 Tips for Designing Logos That Don't Suck," https://designshack.net/articles/inspiration/10-tips-for-designing-logos-that-dont-suck
- *Designhill*: "21 Powerful Tips for Effective Logo Design," https://www.designhill.com/design-blog/powerful-tips-for-effective-logo-design/
- *Wix*: "How to Make a Good Logo: The Dos and Don'ts," https://www.wix.com/blog/2018/07/good-logo-design-tips

While Shopify offers a free logo creation tool called Hatchful (https://hatchful.shopify.com), you'll get the best results if you hire a professional graphic designer from the Shopify

Experts Marketplace (https://experts.shopify.com), which provides referrals for graphic design artists who specialize in creating logos and visual branding for all aspects of ecommerce websites.

You can also find professional freelance graphic designers available for hire on these websites:

- *99designs*: https://99designs.com/designers/search
- *DesignCrowd*: https://www.designcrowd.com/s/logo-design-freelancer
- *Freelancer*: https://www.freelancer.com/find/logo-design
- *LogoOrbit*: https://www.logoorbit.com/
- *Upwork*: https://www.upwork.com/cat/design-creative

For a custom logo, expect to pay at least $100 to $300. Look to hire a graphic designer who will work on a flat-fee basis (as opposed to hourly) and provide you with an initial selection of at least five rough logo designs to choose from. Your fee should include at least two rounds of revisions before you're given the final artwork in digital form.

Make sure the designer guarantees that their work will be 100 percent original and that all legal rights to the logo will be turned over to your business. Depending on the design, you'll then want to register a copyright or trademark for the logo by visiting the pertinent government websites. A filing fee will apply.

However, if you're completely unfamiliar with the registration process, you can hire a company like LegalZoom or an attorney to help you. It's important to legally protect your logo, as well as any intellectual property rights belonging to your company.

Brainstorm a Company Slogan or Tag Line

In one sentence or less, you should be able to communicate a slogan (aka a tag line) that describes what your company does, what it sells, and the core values it represents. You should use this slogan on your website; in your advertising, sales, marketing, and promotional materials; and when you're describing your company to others.

Your company's tag line will become an instrumental aspect of your overall brand, so once again it should resonate with your target audience, be easy to remember, and differentiate your company from the competition.

Shopify offers a free slogan maker to help you brainstorm and compose a tag line (www.shopify.com/tools/slogan-maker). Similar tools are available elsewhere online, such as Squadhelp (https://www.squadhelp.com/taglines) and Oberlo's Slogan Generator (https://www.oberlo.com/tools/slogan-generator). However, if you want the best results, consider hiring a freelance digital marketing specialist or agency that focuses on developing brands for startup ecommerce websites. This is more costly, but if you hire the right person or firm, it's an investment that'll pay off quickly.

Set Up Email Addresses and a Phone Number for Your Business

Once you've chosen your business name and registered a URL, you'll also want to establish email addresses that use that domain name. In addition to setting up individual email accounts for each person who will be helping with your business (e.g., john@yourcompanyname.com), you'll benefit from having more generic email addresses, such as questions@yourcompanyname.com, info@yourcompanyname.com, orders@yourcompanyname.com, and press@yourcompanyname.com.

Your domain name registrar or internet service provider (ISP) can set up these email addresses for you, but other companies can do this on your behalf as well, including:

- *Google Workspace*: https://workspace.google.com/business/signup/welcome
- *Ionos*: https://www.ionos.com/office-solutions/create-an-email-address
- *Microsoft 365*: https://www.microsoft.com/
- *Network Solutions*: https://www.networksolutions.com/email
- *Zoho*: https://www.zoho.com/mail

In some cases, you'll pay a monthly or annual fee per email address. You may be able to get a bundle of 5 or 10 email addresses or even unlimited email addresses for a flat monthly or annual fee, depending on which service you use.

As a business owner, never use a free email address from Google, Microsoft, Apple, Yahoo, or AOL, as they will lessen your company's credibility and do nothing to help your branding.

In addition to a company name, website domain, and business email addresses, you'll also want to set up a separate telephone number for your business and then display this phone number prominently throughout your website. You want to promote the fact that a human is available to answer your customers' questions, address their concerns, and solve their problems.

Most of the people visiting your website will never call you, opting instead to send you an instant message through your site, participate in a real-time online chat (a feature that can be added to your website using a third-party plug-in), or send you an email. But displaying a phone number will help reinforce your company's legitimacy and quickly build credibility with potential customers.

Even better than a traditional phone number for your business is a toll-free (800) number. If you already have a smartphone or landline, you can easily add a second phone number, which will have a different ring and separate voice mail service, so you'll be able to differentiate between personal calls and business calls. Plenty of inexpensive VoIP phone services that allow you to get a phone number (with unlimited incoming and outgoing calls) are also available for a very small fee per month.

When you display a phone number, you can also present your hours of operation, so customers know they can reach you during certain times. If they call after-hours, you will return it on the next business day. By forwarding your business phone number to your smartphone, you can receive business-related calls from virtually anywhere, so you won't be stuck at your desk all day waiting for the phone to ring.

If you want to get fancy, some of the phone services you can get for your business phone number come with a customizable system that allows you to have a message that says something like "Press 1 to place an order, press 2 for customer service, etc." When someone leaves a voice mail, the service can also be set up to transcribe the incoming message and send it to you via email.

The following are just a few of the phone services you can use to get a unique phone number for your business and/or set up a low-cost toll-free phone number for the added credibility it offers in the minds of potential customers.

- *Dialpad*: https://www.dialpad.com/
- *GoTo Connect*: https://www.goto.com/connect
- *Grasshopper*: https://grasshopper.com/
- *RingCentral*: https://www.ringcentral.com/
- *Vonage*: https://www.vonage.com/

Depending on what you're selling and whom you'll be selling to, it might be to your company's advantage to have an answering service (as opposed to a voice mail system) taking your calls 24/7 and then forwarding incoming calls or passing along messages to the proper people.

To set up a relatively inexpensive virtual receptionist service for your business, here are just a few companies you can contact:

- *Abby Connect*: https://www.abby.com/
- *AnswerLive*: https://www.answerlive.com/
- *HelloSells*: https://www.hellosells.com/services/answering-service
- *Ruby*: https://www.ruby.com/
- *VoiceNation*: https://voicenation.com/

Once you determine your phone number and related phone service needs, be sure to shop around for the best deals, based not just on price, but also on the features and services each company offers.

Create a Brand for Your Business

By properly branding your company, you can carefully shape your customers' perceptions by defining what your company stands for and the quality of its products. Your company's brand is a combination of its name, logo, marketing slogan, reputation, customer service, and story. It's essential to develop your brand in a way that truly resonates with your target audience and differentiates your company from its competition in a positive way. At the same time, your company's brand should convey your core values as a business owner (such as honesty, integrity, quality, and top-notch customer service).

Once you've begun to define your company's brand, you should express it throughout all aspects of your business—from the messaging, color scheme, and fonts on your website, emails, blog, and social media content to all printed matter produced by your company (including your letterhead, business cards, brochures, invoices, shipping labels, and product packaging). Brand continuity is vital.

You can start defining your brand during the initial startup phase, although it will likely need to evolve as your company grows and you begin focusing on a broader target audience. Thus, at least every 6 to 12 months, sit down and reevaluate your brand. Make sure it still resonates and helps convey your core message to that audience.

Compose a Business Plan

Traditionally, a business plan is created during a company's startup phase to help educate and attract potential investors. However, even if you plan to fund and operate your ecommerce business on your own, a business plan can still be a valuable tool: It can help you define your business objectives, set long-term goals, determine what products you plan to sell, identify your target audience, establish your company's foundation, and develop a roadmap to follow moving forward.

In a nutshell, a business plan is a document that outlines a company's objectives and strategies and focuses on the steps it'll take to achieve them. It might also include spreadsheets, charts, and graphics to help organize and convey important information. A business plan can help you calculate the financial requirements for your business during the startup phase and moving forward, define your plan for future growth, and attract investors (if necessary).

The SBA (https://www.sba.gov/business-guide/plan-your-business/write-your-business-plan) offers a free tutorial for creating a comprehensive business plan, as well as samples you can use to help format the plan and ensure it includes all the necessary components.

A business plan is typically divided into clearly labeled sections, including the executive summary, company description, market analysis, organization and management description, product line description, marketing and sales plans, and financial projections.

If you're not looking for investors, however, a "lean business plan" will likely work better and be less time-consuming to complete. Be sure to check out the Bplans website (https://articles.bplans.com/an-overview-of-lean-business-planning), which offers information and a free downloadable template for composing a lean business plan.

Shopify offers information about how to create a business plan for your ecommerce website (https://www.shopify.com/blog/business-plan), but countless other books, online tutorials, templates, and tools are available that can make this step in the startup process easier.

For $20 to $40 per month (or $15 to $30 per month when paying annually), an online service called LivePlan (https://www.liveplan.com/) offers an interactive tool for composing a business plan that's specific to your company. Bizplan (https://www.bizplan.com/), GoSmallBiz (https://gosmallbiz.com), and Enloop (https://enloop.com) also sell software and online tools for creating a comprehensive and customized business plan. Once you initially create your business plan, you'll likely need to update it over time as your company grows or your objectives change. This is why it might make sense to subscribe to LivePlan on an annual basis.

Investing time and resources on your business plan early on will help you save time and money moving forward and help you maintain focus as you guide your business toward long-term growth and profitability.

Develop Your Company's Startup Budget and Bookkeeping System

As you put together your business plan, you'll be encouraged to create a startup budget and ongoing operational budget for your business. It's important, right from the start, to determine how much money you'll need to get started, operate your business on a day-to-day basis, and survive until you turn a profit.

Shopify offers some basic bookkeeping tools, but you can easily export the financial data it collects into a well-known bookkeeping or accounting application, such as Intuit's Quick-Books (https://quickbooks.intuit.com). Then you'll be able to prepare and file your tax returns much more easily yourself or share the necessary financial data with your accountant.

Becoming proficient with accounting or bookkeeping software requires a learning curve, especially if you don't have a financial background. However, many books, online tutorials, and other resources are available to help you set up and use these applications. You can also save time by hiring a freelance bookkeeper who is already proficient at using the software.

In addition to QuickBooks, other popular bookkeeping and accounting software options often used by small and ecommerce businesses include:

- *FreshBooks*: https://www.freshbooks.com/
- *NetSuite*: https://www.netsuite.com/
- *Xero*: https://www.xero.com/
- *Zoho Books*: https://www.zoho.com/us/books/bookkeeping-software.html

Register Your Company as a Legal Business Entity

How you establish your company as a legal business entity will have short- and long-term tax and legal ramifications and should be based on a variety of factors, including what you'll be selling online and where you'll be doing business.

The SBA offers an online guide (https://www.sba.gov/) to helping startups understand the differences between the most commonly used business structures. Similar information can be found on LegalZoom's website (https://bit.ly/3NwVBR5). Each structure offers benefits and drawbacks, and they may vary depending on the state where you'll be setting up shop.

While you can research the differences between a sole proprietorship, partnership, DBA (doing business as), LLC (limited liability company), and corporation on your own, once you've put together your business plan, it's a good strategy to have an accountant or attorney review it. They should be able to recommend the best structure for your business from a legal and tax liability standpoint, and then help you complete and submit the required paperwork.

For many ecommerce startups, initially establishing your company as a sole proprietorship (which may also require you to get a DBA or business license) is the easiest and least expensive option, but this does open you up to the most personal liability if your company gets sued. You can always upgrade later to an LLC or corporation as your business grows.

Whichever option you choose, before you start selling anything online, you need to register your company with local, state, and federal authorities (including the IRS) to operate legally. If your company fails to pay taxes and gets caught, you'll face a wide range of fines and interest payments, which potentially could bankrupt you and your business.

Set Up Your Home Office

Establishing your business on paper and then creating its online presence are both necessary steps in the startup process, but you'll also need to set up an office in the real world where you can run your business, store your inventory (if applicable), and fulfill your orders. You can rent office or warehouse space if needed, but at least initially you'll probably want to set up a homebased business.

This means dedicating space in your home for an office. On the plus side, operating a home office will qualify you for tax deductions, so be sure to speak with your accountant about this.

When choosing the location for your home office, you might opt for a spare bedroom, attic, basement, garage, walk-in closet, or corner of your living room or master bedroom. While you don't want your home office to infringe too much on your everyday living space, especially if you have a family, you also want to make sure the space you choose is well-lit, temperature controlled, large enough, quiet, and equipped with sufficient electrical outlets and internet connectivity.

At the core of your home office is your main work space, which should consist of a large desk and an adjustable, ergonomic office chair. The chair should allow you to sit and work comfortably for many hours at a time without experiencing neck, shoulder, arm, wrist, or lower-back pain.

A brand-new office chair that meets these requirements can be quite costly. A new Herman Miller Aeron chair (https://store.hermanmiller.com/office-chairs-aeron/aeron-chair/2195348.html), for example, will set you back nearly $1,700. However, if you buy used from Facebook Marketplace, eBay, or a furniture reseller, you could pay as little as $300 for the same chair. So take your time and shop around.

In addition to your desk and chair, you'll need proper lighting, file/supply cabinets, and some core business equipment, such as a computer, printer, scanner, and telephone (or smartphone). If you don't want to be confined to your desk throughout the business day, consider investing in a laptop (as opposed to a desktop computer); to save space and money, purchase an all-in-one printer that includes printing, scanning, photocopying, and faxing capabilities.

The latest all-in-one inkjet printers use ink tanks, as opposed to ink cartridges, so you'll save money over time by not having to constantly buy replacement cartridges.

In addition to your main printer, a separate shipping label printer is also a worthwhile expense, especially if you'll be filling more than a handful of orders each day. One company called ShipStation (https://info.shipstation.com/print-shipping-labels) offers a comprehensive application and label printer designed to meet the needs of small to midsize ecommerce businesses. The ShipStation software links directly with Shopify to import order data, and then creates shipping labels and postage (if applicable) to ship via the USPS, UPS, FedEx, or DHL.

Your office will need several electrical outlets (so you don't have to run extension cords around your home or overload a single outlet or power strip). You'll also want to ensure that the signal from your home's wifi is strong enough where you'll be working. If not, you could install a wifi signal booster, along with a state-of-the-art wifi router and modem that offers the fastest signal and most reliable internet connection possible. A number of free online tools are available that allow you to measure your current internet speed, so you can make sure you're getting the connection you're paying for. Two such tools can be found at M-Lab's Speed Test (https://speed.measurementlab.net) and Speedcheck (https://www.speedcheck.org/).

In addition to all this, you'll likely need a suite of software applications to help you perform common work-related tasks like word processing, spreadsheet management, email management, scheduling, video calling, bookkeeping, photo or video editing, package shipping, and inventory management.

The Microsoft 365 suite (https://www.microsoft.com/en-us/microsoft-365), Apple iWork (https://www.apple.com/iwork/), or Google Workspace (https://workspace.google.com) apps will provide most of the core software and cloud-based tools you'll need, along with the tools Shopify offers. A free alternative for core applications like word processing and spreadsheet management is Apache OpenOffice (https://www.openoffice.org/).

In addition to your main work area, a portion of your home office may need to be set aside to store your inventory in an out-of-the-way but climate-controlled space. You'll also need space to set up your "shipping department," from which you can package and fulfill your orders.

Within this designated shipping area, you'll likely need to maintain a supply of boxes, packing tape and other packaging materials, shipping labels, a postage scale, a way to print postage or shipping labels for UPS, FedEx, etc., and a work space where you can fill the orders and then store your packages until they're picked up by the shipping company.

Meanwhile, if you plan to take your own product photos or videos or create your own social media content or podcast, you'll also need to set up an in-home studio with backdrops, lighting, and camera or video equipment, as well as recording equipment if you are producing a podcast.

In the end, how you lay out your work space is a matter of personal preference, but it should be comfortable, clean, and quiet, and allow you to focus on whatever you're doing throughout your workday.

SHOPIFY EXPERT

Kristin Berry Mastoras
Founder of Miss Design Berry and Kiki and Max

Kristin Berry Mastoras is a skilled artist, illustrator, and graphic designer who sells her artwork on all sorts of products through her two Shopify-based stores. She operates two distinct online businesses because the products she sells on each cater to entirely different target audiences.

While working as an illustrator for an advertising agency, Mastoras created an online shop using Etsy to sell some of her original artwork to earn some extra money. Over the next several years growing her Etsy-based business, it reached a point where she needed more from the website, because her goal was to quit her advertising agency job and become a full-time online business operator.

From Etsy, she moved her business to Squarespace, and then hired a website designer to help her establish her business using WordPress. However, the functionality she was looking for was not offered by any of these ecommerce platforms, so in 2016 she hired a different agency that specializes just in creating Shopify-based stores. The agency then helped her build and launch Miss Design Berry using the Shopify platform (shown in Figure 4.1 on page 61).

Miss Design Berry caters to people planning a wedding. However, once someone gets married, they often want to continue using the company's services for things

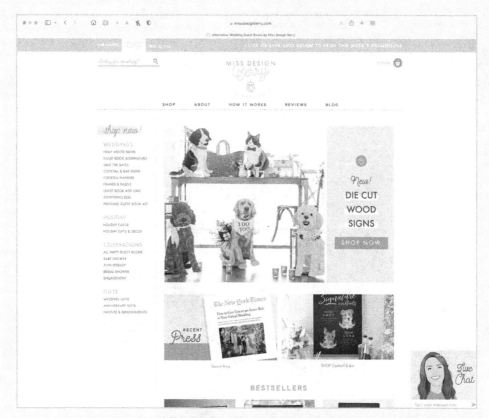

FIGURE 4.1 The Miss Design Berry home page is shown here.

like baby showers and decorating a nursery. Because selling services and art related to weddings and wedding décor is so different from selling services and art related to babies, Mastoras opened a second Shopify-based store called Kiki and Max (shown in Figure 4.2 on page 62).

Q: *Do you operate your businesses yourself, or do you have people who help you?*

I have a team of talented women who work with me remotely. Once Miss Design Berry was fully operational, we duplicated the core design and infrastructure of that online business to create and launch Kiki and Max. These two companies have totally separate brands, and we market them using different advertising and marketing strategies, but it's the same team that runs both businesses simultaneously, which makes the whole shopping process much more straightforward for our customers.

FIGURE 4.2 The Kiki and Max home page is shown here. Notice the format is very similar to her other online business, but the product offerings are different, as is the target audience for this business.

Q: *Selling products to people getting married is a broad audience. What have you done to establish a niche?*

While some of our products will appeal to anyone planning a wedding, and almost all are customizable, we also have begun offering more niche-oriented products to people who want to include their pets in their wedding festivities, for example. The more niche the products we offer are, the better they sell because we're able to reach a targeted audience for them so much easier.

Initially, we sought out first-time customers for the Miss Design Berry company, but then relied on repeat business from those customers to make Kiki and Max successful. Since most people only have one big wedding in their lifetime, they only shop from Miss Design Berry once in conjunction with that event. However,

Kiki and Max allows us to maintain relationships with those customers and have them become repeat customers multiple times in the future, whether they want baby products and baby shower items for themselves or to give as gifts. We look at Kiki and Max as a lifestyle family brand, so the client relationship we have is very different from Miss Design Berry.

Q: *Generating repeat business can be a huge challenge for an ecommerce business operator. What is your best advice for being able to achieve this with as many customers as possible?*

We are sticklers for the service we provide to our clients. One of the best tools we use to offer superior service is a real-time (live) chat through the website. Our products are all custom-made, so our clients tend to have a lot of questions. Allowing them to click on a button and be able to chat live with us allows us to build a stronger relationship with each customer and better cater to their wants, needs, and concerns. We also use this as a tool for telling our customers about add-ons and upgrades to their order that they might be interested in, which often leads to higher sales volume from each customer.

Our live chat feature allows customers to converse with a knowledgeable human, as opposed to an AI-driven bot. This service is not available 24 hours a day, but we do offer extended hours. On the website itself, we often offer an exclusive discount to people who use the chat feature, because I know that once we engage them in a chat, the conversion rate for transforming that visitor into a paying customer will be much higher.

Q: *What would you say is the biggest misconception you had when you first decided to migrate your online business to the Shopify platform?*

After trying several different ecommerce platforms, I did not realize just how customizable a Shopify-based ecommerce website can be, especially when you hire a programmer to alter a theme. Shopify is a set of tools for building your own thing, and it's currently used by some of the biggest companies in the world, so it's extremely scalable.

Q: *It seems like you have invested a lot of time and resources in establishing your company's brand. How did you do this initially, and what advice do you have for other startups when it comes to branding an ecommerce website?*

Our brand for each business started with a look, a logo, and a color scheme that extends throughout everything we do. We also have a voice and a tone that we use in all our copy, and this extends to all the interactions we have with our clients. Each website's About page, for example, introduces customers to our team and explains exactly what values we represent. I believe people care about a brand, but they also really care about who the people are behind the brand, and that makes it easier for people to quickly connect with what we're offering.

I believe a company's brand always goes through a level of evolution over time. The brand I created when I started my Etsy-based business 11 years ago is almost unrecognizable to what it is today, although core components of the brand remain the same. I am a strong believer that the people operating a business need to connect with it and truly believe in their products and services, and then have a compelling story to tell that will capture the attention of customers in a positive and upbeat way. Part of this story should explain how you do what you do, but more importantly, why you're doing it.

While you can easily update a logo or color scheme, for instance, you should not need to change the core values that your company represents and operates under. In terms of giving the website a visual update, we do this every season, often in conjunction with the launch of new products. This allows us to keep the site fresh. We also display reviews on the site, which are constantly being updated, and we make a conscious effort to continuously publish new and fresh content on our social media feeds.

To manage and display customer reviews on our websites, we use the Judge.me app [https://judge.me] that works in conjunction with Shopify. I believe publishing reviews for our products on the website goes a long way to helping build our reputation and credibility.

Our products tend to be high-end and somewhat expensive, and when we poll customers and ask why they decided to shop from us initially, the response is almost always because of the positive reviews and ratings that related to our products and our customer service. We don't just try to please customers with our products and customer service, we strive to blow them away, and this sets us apart from our competition and allows us to charge higher prices.

Q: *You mentioned that your products are priced at a premium level, and one way you justify this is with superior reviews. What else do you do to make your customers feel good about spending more for what you offer?*

We offer a higher level of interaction with our clients, and after a client places an order, we are available by telephone or live chat to converse with them. We're also really, really dedicated to the quality of our artwork and the level of detail in what we offer. We do what we do well, and we do it better than everyone else. One reason why I left Etsy is because most businesses on there are forced to compete on price, offer a fast turnaround, and offer free shipping. For us to do things right, we take longer and need to charge more, and our customers are willing to pay for that added value and level of service.

One thing I really like about Shopify is that it allows us to build and create the shopping experience we want for our customers. It's hard at first for a company to establish themselves as a premium brand, especially since most sellers start off selling online as a hobby. A hobby ecommerce model is not sustainable as a true business model. If you treat your business as a hobby, it will always be a hobby. It won't start performing like a business until you treat it like a business.

If you truly believe in what you're selling, the price point you set will set the level of expectation your customers will have for the products. If you set a high price point and then deliver on those expectations, you won't have any problem charging higher prices.

Q: *Because your products are custom-made for your clients, you promote a five-week lead time between ordering and delivery. How do you educate your customers about this?*

We make it very clear in multiple places on the website that everything is custom done for each customer and that due to demand, the lead time can be up to five weeks. We do, however, charge extra for rush delivery, which allows people to jump to the front of the line, so to speak. Especially during the off-season, however, we always do whatever we can to deliver orders quicker than the time frame we promise.

Q: *Based on your own experience, when someone is starting to sell online via a Shopify-based website, what are some of the key skills they'll need to master early on?*

One of the biggest things that people overlook is the text that they incorporate into their website, within their product listings, and on all other website pages. You don't necessarily need to hire a professional copywriter, but you do need to invest a lot of time and effort into composing and proofreading your text, and then studying how your target customers react to it.

I have personally taken several online copywriting courses, which have been very helpful. Ecommerce business operators don't always initially understand how important their product headlines and descriptions are and how much they impact someone's buying decision. Also, even if you're still developing your brand, you need a website that looks professional. If someone visits your website for the first time and it looks unprofessional, fishy, or scammy, they'll simply click away.

I recommend focusing a lot on your product descriptions and the product photography, but also on customizing your selected Shopify theme, so it does not look generic and like hundreds of other websites. Take time to select your color scheme and focus on how everything flows together. The instant vibe a visitor gets in the first few seconds of visiting your website will be a huge factor in whether they choose to stay and then buy something.

I am also a big fan of showcasing social proof on the website by displaying customer ratings and reviews, and in tying the company's Instagram feed to the website, for example. Early on, when I started using Shopify, I added an app that displayed a pop-up window that included a message saying, "John from New York just purchased . . ." This helped to add a sense of legitimacy to the business and showed new visitors that other people were placing orders.

Q: *As a professional graphic designer, do you think it's necessary for a startup ecommerce business to make its website look amazing?*

It all depends on your budget. If you only have a few hundred dollars to spend, invest in a professional-looking company logo and in a nice template that you can customize yourself. If you have a few thousand dollars to spend, then hire a professional graphic designer and/or website designer who will make your site look amazing. You can always upgrade your site once you start generating a profit, but right from the start the website needs to look professional.

Early on, I never had the space to set up my own in-house photography studio to create my own photography for the website, so I have always worked with a professional photographer. On top of that, I have always asked my clients to share their own photos of my products in use, which we display on the website, and that too goes a long way in helping to increase future sales. Both of our websites include a client gallery page, which is dedicated to showcasing real photos of our products taken and shared by past customers.

Q: *By looking at both of your websites, it's obvious that you've made the choice to keep your core menu options simple. On the Kiki and Max site, the main menu* *options are Shop, About, Reviews, and Blog. What do you think are the most important pages to showcase on an ecommerce website?*

I think a lot of companies skip the About page, or they don't tell a compelling story using this area of an ecommerce website. I believe that if someone is thinking about shopping on a website they've never been to before, they want to get to know the people behind the company as well as its story. This is how the About page should be used. Figure out what your target audience really values about the companies they opt to do business with, and then share that information on the About page. Tell people why you do what you do and what made you want to do it, and explain what sets your business and products apart and why you believe so much in what you're doing.

Q: *Is there any other advice you'd like to share with ecommerce business operators who are first getting started?*

It can be very overwhelming to start building a Shopify-based ecommerce store and then worry that it's not perfect. One of the important lessons I have learned is that you just need to do the very best you can to get something professional-looking out there. You can then tweak and improve upon it as you go, based on the feedback you get from customers and clients.

The Next Step: Start Creating Your Company's Ecommerce Website

With the infrastructure of your company and its foundation now firmly in place, and with a business plan that'll keep you focused and on track, it's time to tap the power of Shopify to begin designing, branding, and populating your ecommerce website. This is the focus of Chapter 5, "Creating Your Online Store."

Creating Your Online Store

This chapter focuses on gathering the custom assets you'll need to import (i.e., drag and drop) into your Shopify-based ecommerce website as you're designing and creating it. It will also help you determine how to organize and present that content and provide Shopify with the appropriate information, so that you wind up with a professional-looking, well-branded, easy-to-navigate, informative, and compelling website.

As you know, Shopify is a constantly evolving platform, so instead of offering step-by-step directions for creating your online store, which would be out-of-date quickly, we'll talk here about the key steps and strategies you should implement while designing your website. The actual Shopify interface is rather straightforward, so if you already know how to use a word processor and web browser, you should have little trouble navigating your way through the process. The key is to showcase the right information in the best way possible, so you can attract and impress your target audience.

Essential Pages and Content Your Website Should Include

Like any website, your ecommerce website should be divided into sections and pages that make it easy for a visitor to quickly find the information they're looking for. If someone must spend more than a few seconds looking for your product descriptions, your return policy, or your contact information, you've done something wrong.

Let's look at the most important elements of an ecommerce website. These pages (or sections) include the following:

About Us

The About Us section is where you should tell your company's story and profile the people who founded or play a large role in the operation of your business or who invented the products you sell. The goal is to make your business more personal, set it apart from your competition, and share information that'll help build loyalty among your customers.

A few of the questions that the About Us section should answer include:

- Why did you start the business, and why are you passionate about its products?
- What is your company philosophy, and what is its mission?
- What sets your business apart from its competitors?

You can also use the About Us section to share other relevant information, such as your company's affiliation with a charity, or offer a behind-the-scenes look at how it operates (or how your products are made).

The About Us section should be primarily text-based, concise, and compellingly written. However, when appropriate, you can also use photos, video clips, or other branding materials to help tell the story. The approach and tone should cater to your target audience, using terminology and language they'll understand and relate to.

Contact Us

You can present the Contact Us function on your website in a number of different ways, such as:

- Display a menu button on your page, which takes visitors directly to a contact form that will send you an email
- Prominently display your phone number and email address on every page of your website
- Offer a live text-messaging/chat feature that allows visitors to communicate with you immediately and in real time

The goal is to make yourself accessible, so a website visitor will feel confident that a human is available to them if they have any questions, run into problems, or have any concerns about what you're selling.

FAQ (Frequently Asked Questions)

Once you launch your site, you will be repeatedly asked a series of common questions about your company and its products—about your return policy, shipping options, the available sizes and colors of your products, and so on.

Depending on what you're selling and to whom you're selling, these questions will vary. But the goal of the FAQ is to answer these questions in a quick, easily accessible, and straightforward format.

Initially, based on your knowledge of your products and target audience, anticipate what the most common questions will be and answer them. Then, as you start interacting with your customers, update the FAQ to answer at least 10 of the questions they ask you most often.

Be sure to make it clear that if someone needs more information, they should contact you directly by phone, email, or text message—whichever way you prefer to interact with website visitors.

Product Showcase (Product Listings)

Without a doubt, the most important part of your ecommerce website is where you showcase the products you're selling. A product listing will include text giving details about the product along with photos. You can also include video clips and product reviews.

Since potential buyers can't try out, touch, or physically examine what you're selling, it's up to your product listings to inform visitors about each product, explain how it addresses their needs or solves a problem, and get them excited to acquire it. Your website visitors have a very short attention span, so you must do this in a clear, concise, and attention-grabbing way, telling them as much as possible about what you're selling as quickly as you can.

The text in each product description should be accurate, informative, upbeat, and attention-grabbing, while not giving readers any false expectations. The photos (and videos) you include should showcase the product clearly, allowing visitors to see it up close, from various angles, and see the quality and detail the product offers. As we said in Chapter 3, "What Can Be Sold Online," mix-and-match product photography (which showcases your product with a simple background) with lifestyle photography (which shows the product being used in the real world).

Keep in mind that the title, description, photo captions, and other information in each product listing should include SEO-friendly keywords that describe each product, using terms your prospective customers will most likely use when searching for what you're selling.

Shopping Cart

Once someone clicks on the Buy Button for one of your product listings, that item will be added to their shopping cart. This is the section of the website where you'll collect their name, email address, payment information, billing and shipping addresses, shipping preferences, coupon/promo code (if applicable), and any other information you'll need to process and ship the order.

Shopify has done an amazing job at making it easy for you to create a shopping cart and checkout experience that's professional, straightforward, and easy to navigate. But as you're customizing this section, be sure you don't clutter it by asking too many irrelevant questions or adding content that will slow down the checkout process.

The moment a visitor gets confused, distracted, or delayed during the checkout process, they will give up, abandon the shopping cart, and go somewhere else. When providing customers with checkout options, keep things as simple as possible.

Within the shopping cart, you can add incentives for your visitors, such as free shipping, or use optional Shopify apps to showcase recommendations for additional products, product bundles, or add-ons they might be interested in (offered at a discount), based on items they've added to their shopping cart. Just be cautious with these.

Using another optional Shopify app, adding shopping cart recovery functionality can be a powerful sales tool, if you use it without harassing your website visitors. This feature will email anyone who starts to check out on your website but for whatever reason abandons their cart before it's finalized. In this email (or series of emails), you can emphasize the value and quality of your products and provide an incentive (such as a discount) if they click on the provided link and finish their purchase.

Some of the optional apps you can use for this purpose include:

- *Abandoned Cart Recovery Email*: https://apps.shopify.com/care-cart
- *Carti Abandoned Cart Recovery*: https://apps.shopify.com/carti-recover-cart-abandonment
- *iCart Cart Drawer Cart Upsell*: https://apps.shopify.com/icart
- *Rivo Abandoned Cart Recovery*: https://apps.shopify.com/push-notification-hero
- *Smart Cart Recovery*: https://apps.shopify.com/smart-cart-recovery

Ratings and Reviews

Using optional Shopify apps, it's relatively easy to add a Customer Ratings and Reviews feature to your website and to product listings. When you can showcase an abundance of positive ratings and reviews, it instantly helps establish your company's reputation and makes potential customers feel more confident about purchasing specific products.

Ratings on a website are typically star based (between one and five stars, with five stars being the highest rating). In addition to seeing how many individual star ratings a product or merchant has received, an average star-based rating is also typically displayed. This is calculated based on the number of ratings received and is a quick indication of what a large group of people think about a merchant or product. When someone sees a product has received an average rating of 4.8 stars based on hundreds or thousands of ratings, they will have a lot of confidence that what they're about to buy is of high quality.

Reviews on a website are typically written by customers who have previously purchased the product. They're usually between a few sentences and a few paragraphs long and delve deeper into what the customer really likes (or dislikes) about the product and/ or merchant. Online shoppers who like to invest a little extra time doing research about a product before they buy it will spend a few extra minutes reading a handful of product/ merchant reviews.

Remember, though, once you decide to display ratings and reviews on your website, you have no ability to edit or alter whatever ratings or reviews you receive. If you're not 100 percent confident that your products and customer service will receive top-notch ratings and reviews, do not implement this functionality, as low ratings and poor reviews will quickly tarnish your company's reputation and drive potential customers away.

Press/Media

If you intend to use public relations as a marketing tool for your business and encourage the media (newspapers, magazines, radio shows, TV shows, blogs, podcasts, YouTubers, etc.) to include your company and its products in their editorial coverage, you'll want a Press/ Media section on your website.

This section should showcase press coverage and positive product reviews your company has already received (again, to boost your company's credibility). It should also make all your press materials (press releases, company background information, product photos, and other useful content) available to members of the media interested in covering your company and its products. You should also include contact information in case the media want to speak to you directly.

Anytime you receive an inquiry from a member of the working media, respond immediately and provide whatever additional information, interviews, or product samples for review they request, as they're probably working under a tight deadline.

Social Media Links

If you're using your company's social media presence as a sales and marketing tool or to create an interactive online community around your brand and your products, it makes sense to showcase some of this content on your ecommerce website—or at least include links to your social media feeds. However, anytime you're taking visitors away from your website (even if it's for something positive), always open that content in a separate browser window, so that your company's website will remain accessible.

Newsletter, Blog, or Podcast

Many ecommerce businesses find that publishing a weekly or monthly newsletter, blog, or podcast is a powerful sales and marketing tool that allows them to build a closer relationship with existing and potential customers. If you decide to use one of these tools, promote it heavily on your website and either embed the content there or provide links to the content for website visitors to easily access it.

Branding Is Essential

As you're creating each part of your website, branding and consistency are essential. Use the same tone, messaging, color scheme, fonts and styles, layout, and overall design throughout your website.

Remember, when creating your Shopify website, you'll initially select a theme that you'll then be able to customize with the various website sections, pages, and functionality to provide the best online shopping experience possible. How you customize the theme and what functionality you add (including the Shopify apps you utilize) is entirely up to you. Choose a theme that nicely fits your brand, and then customize it in a way that'll appeal specifically to your target audience, while focusing on the key messaging you've composed.

Putting the Pieces Together

Once you've composed, created, and collected the content and assets you plan to add to your ecommerce website, it's time to set up your Shopify account and start building your site using the tools offered by Shopify and customizing your shop with your own content. The quickest way to do this is to open your favorite web browser on your desktop or laptop, visit https://www.shopify.com/online, and click on the Start Free Trial button in the top-right corner of the browser window (as well as in a couple of other places on the page).

As you can see in Figure 5.1 below, you start by entering your email address, creating an account password, and providing the name of your store. Your store's name will be used to create a unique website URL that uses the YourStoreName.myshopify.com format. You

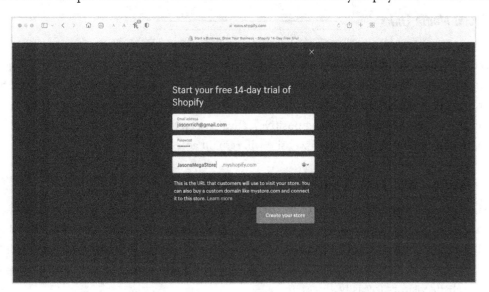

FIGURE 5.1 Start by creating your Shopify account.

can then forward your company's domain name (YourCompanyName.com) to this Shopify website address.

When you set up your Shopify account, you'll be given a free 14-day trial and can begin creating your online store without providing any payment information. However, you will not be able to start selling anything from your website until you set up a paid account with Shopify.

The next step is to complete a short questionnaire that will help Shopify provide you with the best tools, based on your goals. Each question is accompanied by a pull-down menu of responses to choose from.

These initial questions include:

- Are you already selling?
- What is your current revenue?
- Which industry will you be operating in?

For the first question, if you state that you're not yet selling any products, you'll be asked an additional series of targeted questions about whether you plan to use a dropshipping service to sell your products and what types of products you plan to sell (shown in Figure 5.2 below). They

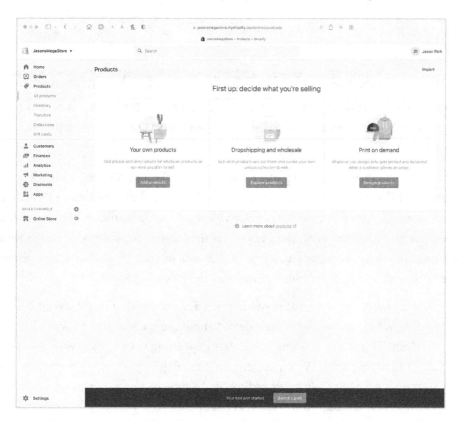

FIGURE 5.2 Every step in the Shopify website creation process involves you following a step-by-step format. In some cases, you'll be asked to answer simple questions.

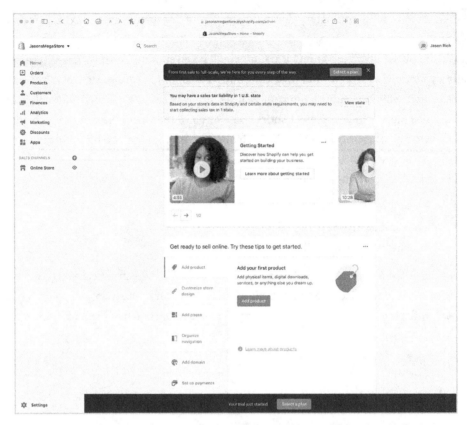

FIGURE 5.3 From this main dashboard, you have access to the tools needed to create, publish, and manage your online business using the Shopify platform.

will also ask if you plan to sell using other sales channels through Shopify, such as Facebook, Instagram, and Google, or if you plan to use the Shopify Buy Button within your other content.

Following this, you'll be asked to provide your name, address, phone number, and business website URL. At this point, the site will create the shell for your ecommerce website. When viewing the main dashboard, along the left side of your browser window (shown in Figure 5.3 above), you'll see a menu that includes the following options:

- *Home*: This command returns you to the main Shopify dashboard screen.
- *Orders*: When you receive orders, details about them are displayed here.
- *Products*: This screen is where you'll start populating your website with product listings and descriptions. Which option you'll use depends on whether you'll be selling your own products, using a dropshipping service, or using a print-on-demand service to create and ship your orders. The submenu gives you tools to create individual product listings, manage your inventory, create product collections, and generate digital gift cards.

- *Customers*: This is a CRM (customer relationship management) application that's built into Shopify. It allows you to manage details about your customers and their purchase history.
- *Finances*: Click here to see how your business is performing, and how much revenue it's earning (as this pertains to your ecommerce website and online selling activities through Shopify).
- *Analytics*: See real-time and extremely detailed information about traffic to your website, sales, your online store conversion rate, average order value, returning customer rate, and other details that will help you determine what is and isn't working in terms of your website's content and your overall sales, advertising, and marketing efforts.
- *Marketing*: Discover and use a wide range of tools to advertise and market your business, including social media, email marketing, text message marketing, abandoned checkout tools, and online advertising options.
- *Discounts*: From here, you can manage various types of discounts or promotions you'd like to share with your site's visitors, including discount codes and automatic discounts.
- *Apps*: Browse the Shopify App Store and start finding apps to add functionality to your website.
- *Online Store*: From this menu option, you can create, edit, and manage components of your ecommerce website, including individual pages, themes, visitor-accessible menu options, navigation functionality, and related preferences. You can also preview your store (both the live version and the draft version) and measure its loading speed and speed score.

At any point during the 14-day trial, you can select a Shopify plan (shown in Figure 5.4 on page 78) to fully activate your account. To do this, click on the Select a Plan option that's offered as a menu option. As of early 2022, these options included Basic ($29 per month), Shopify ($79 per month), or Advanced ($299 per month). What's included with each plan and the ongoing or per-sale fees associated with each plan are listed on the Shopify website at https://www.shopify.com/pricing.

Start Creating Product Listings

From the main dashboard page, begin by creating, composing, and developing each of your separate product pages (or listings). To do this, simply click on the Add Product option. As you're completing the form to generate a product listing (shown in Figure 5.5 on page 79), only provide the specific information requested in each field. Do not improvise and try adding information or content on your own. Shopify requires you to follow a specific format when inputting product information to ensure your product listings will be displayed properly and be searchable.

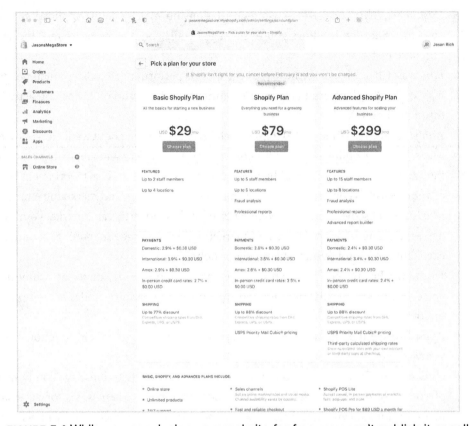

FIGURE 5.4 While you can design your website for free, you can't publish it or sell anything until you sign up and pay for a Shopify plan. As of early 2022, three main plans were available.

Start with the Title field by composing a compelling, descriptive, and attention-grabbing title for each product listing, using SEO-related search terms as appropriate. Next, compose the Description. Notice that you can format the text using bold, italics, and underlining. You can also adjust the color and alignment of the text, a numbered or bulleted list, and/or a table. What content you add here should all be used to convey as much information about what you're selling in the most concise but informative way possible.

Next you should add the Media for the product listing. This can be photos, videos, illustrations, or computer-generated 3D models. The goal is to showcase the product, its details, and its features in the best way possible.

Other information you'll be asked to enter includes your item's Pricing, Inventory, and Shipping details, as well as custom information, if applicable. This is information you deem important about your product that specific fields offered by Shopify have not requested. Other details about a product that you're able to include, in fields displayed below the Organization heading, include the product's Vendor, Product Type,

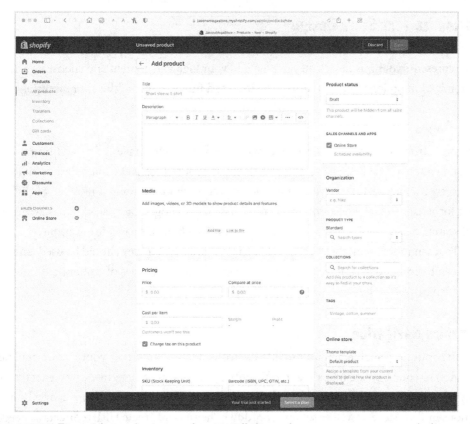

FIGURE 5.5 For each product you plan to sell through your ecommerce website, you'll need to complete this product listing form on Shopify. Be as specific as you can and be sure to add the requested information in each field.

and whether you want to add it to a specific Collection. For each listing, you can immediately add it to your website by adjusting the Product Status to Active or leave it in Draft mode until you're ready to publish the product on your site. A Collection is a group of products that are related and that the same customer might be interested in purchasing at the same time.

One extremely important field you'll need to fill in for each product listing is Tags. These are keywords or search terms you believe people will use when looking for the product. These should be SEO-related terms that are descriptive and relevant to the product. When you've filled in all the appropriate fields for each product listing, click on the Save button to save your content and add it to your website. For gold earrings, tags might include: earring, gold, jewelry, 14K gold, etc.

You'll need to create separate, well-written, and informative product listings for each product you plan to sell on your website, along with related artwork (photos, videos, etc.). Take your time creating this content and proofread everything carefully.

Customize Your Store Design

Click on this option from the main Shopify dashboard to browse themes and choose one that best represents your business. You can then add your logo and content and choose a variety of customization options that will impact the look and functionality of the entire website.

Add Pages

As you learned earlier in this chapter, your website should have a few additional pages beyond your product listings. The Shopify Page Builder (which is the main design tool you'll use to create and customize your site) allows you to choose among a number of different page formats: product, collection, collections list, pages, blog, blog post, cart, password, 404, and search. Select the Pages option here to create an About Us page, for example.

To learn more about these page formatting options, when they should be used, and how they can be incorporated into your website to share different types of content and information, visit https://bit.ly/3amOhJI.

Organize Navigation

Use the options available here to provide the icons, menus, and tools your visitors will need to navigate your website quickly and efficiently. The goal is to help them find exactly what they're seeking with the least effort possible. From here, you can add, remove, or edit menu options in your store as well as set up drop-down menus and create URL redirects as needed.

The appearance of menus, buttons, and pull-down menus will be determined by the Shopify theme you select, and then by how you customize that theme.

Add Domain Details

When you establish your trial Shopify account, you're assigned a website URL that uses the YourStoreName.myshopify.com format. Using the tools in this section of the dashboard, you can add one or more of your own registered domain names and forward them to your Shopify store's home page or to specific pages on the website.

Set Up Payment Options

The central purpose of an ecommerce website is to allow you to accept and process orders, so you will need to accept payment options. Here, you can link your own credit card merchant account details (through your bank or another financial institution) to your website, activate Shopify's own payment processing options, and/or set up electronic payment service functionality (such as PayPal or Apple Pay).

If you're in the United States and choose to take advantage of Shopify's payment processing options, right from the start you'll be able to accept Visa, Mastercard, American

Express, Discover, and Diners Club debit and credit cards. Depending on which options you select, per-sale fees may apply.

Meanwhile, if you'll be selling to a global audience, you can set up the ability to accept foreign currencies and credit/debit cards issued to consumers in other countries.

Before you can get paid for your online sales, however, you must first set up your company's Shopify Payments account, which will require linking your company's banking information to the account. This must be done within 21 days of receiving your first sale, but it should be done immediately upon setting up your website (before it goes live). To do this, from the Shopify admin page, select Settings, and then Payments. Choose the Complete Account Setup option in the Shopify Payments section.

Set Up and Review Shipping Details

Shopify allows you to work with major shippers (USPS, UPS, DHL) to fulfill your orders and send your products to customers. As you're creating your website, you'll need to decide what shipping options you plan to offer to your customers (ground shipping, two-day shipping, overnight shipping, international shipping, Priority Mail shipping, etc.), and then which shipping services you plan to use.

You'll then need to set up the tools to calculate shipping charges, based on the options you select (if applicable), or opt to offer free shipping to customers. Once this is done, you can use other tools to automatically generate shipping labels, customer receipts, and packing slips. However, you must define your shipping strategy so you understand all the added costs involved and then accurately build those expenses into your operating budget.

For additional information about shipping options for a Shopify-based ecommerce website, visit https://bit.ly/3aG8jz6.

Localize Your Store for International Shoppers

Shopify offers a variety of tools to help your website appeal to international shoppers. You can have the text on your website automatically translated into different languages, you can localize your store for different regions, and you can accept foreign currencies as payment. Much of this can be accomplished through adding Shopify apps to your website. Follow this link to see what apps are available to help your site appeal to shoppers from abroad: https://bit.ly/3mdbS2k.

Make Sure Everything Is Perfect Before Publishing—Shopify Can Help

As you complete each section of the Shopify dashboard and create the content that will be added to various pages of your website, you'll discover a vast selection of free tutorials and blog posts on Shopify explaining exactly how to use each of the features and functions available to you. Take advantage of these resources and develop a thorough understanding of the Shopify platform as you go. Here's a good place to start: https://www.shopify.com/partners/blog/topics/shopify-tutorials.

Shopify also hosts its own YouTube channel (https://bit.ly/3taGfdl), where you can find easy-to-understand and informative video tutorials that cover just about every feature, function, and tool offered by the platform. The Shopify website also offers a robust Help section, which offers free articles and how-to information. You can find it here: https://help.shopify.com/en.

To ensure you've put all the pieces of your website together properly and checked off all the steps needed to launch a successful ecommerce store, take advantage of Shopify's free "General Checklist for Starting a New Shopify Store," which you'll find here: https://bit.ly/3t9qfsj.

Just as important, be sure to triple-check everything and have multiple people proofread and fact-check all the content on your website, and then check the functionality of everything before the website goes live. Do not simply rely on a spelling and grammar checker.

At this point, you'll also want to test every aspect of your website using multiple web browsers (including Microsoft Edge, Google Chrome, Apple Safari, Firefox, Samsung Internet, and Opera), and make sure your website looks good and functions properly on both desktop and laptop computers, as well as on tablets and smartphones (both Android and Apple's iOS). Everything should auto format and look professional, regardless of the screen size.

Focus on Your Chosen Theme and Optional Apps

This chapter provided an overview of the many steps involved in the website-building process using Shopify. It's essential to take your time and review each option offered by each menu to ensure you're providing the right information in the appropriate place. You'll also need to handle some back-end tasks associated with the operation of your website, such as linking your banking information, setting up email accounts, and adjusting your store-management settings.

One of the worst mistakes you can make at this point is rushing the process or attempting to take shortcuts just to get your business launched faster. You don't want to make careless mistakes that could drive customers away or that will be time-consuming and costly to fix later. Many of the choices you must make during the website design and creation process will be specific to your business and its brand and should cater to the wants and needs of your target audience, so stay focused on that.

Refrain from adding features, functions, or buying options that will confuse, annoy, or distract your visitors or that will be counterproductive to your goal of converting visitors into paying customers and then into repeat customers. As a rule, keep your layout, design, and navigation options as simple and clutter-free as possible.

At the same time, make your product offerings as straightforward as you can, requiring customers to make the least number of decisions and provide the least amount of personal information possible to place their order and have it processed quickly.

Two of the biggest things that set Shopify apart from other ecommerce platforms are the vast selection of themes you can choose from, allowing you to customize the appearance and functionality of your website, and the equally vast selection of optional apps you can use to add specific features and functions to your store. The focus of the next chapter is on finding and choosing the best theme, and then selecting the most appropriate apps to integrate into your website (without making it more confusing for your visitors).

SHOPIFY EXPERT

Zoë Chapman
Inventor of the Whizzer and Founder of Shopify-Based Kiddiwhizz

Every parent knows the frustration of having a small child who always seems to need a restroom at the most inopportune times. To address this parenting dilemma, in 2014 Zoë Chapman (a very determined single parent in the UK) came up with the Whizzer—the first handheld unisex toilet for kids. After having to put the project on hold several times due to life- and parenting-related challenges, online presales for the Whizzer began in early 2021.

Leading up to the Whizzer's launch, Chapman single-handedly designed every element of the product (including its packaging), learned every business essential from the legal protection of inventions to the manufacturing process, created a rather impressive Shopify-based ecommerce website (https://kiddiwhizz.com), and handled the advertising, marketing, and PR campaign for the product and company.

Since the website went live on February 17, 2021, the response has been overwhelming. Chapman now runs Kiddiwhizz as a homebased business selling her product to parents in the UK, and she is planning to expand worldwide. You can see the home page for the website in Figure 5.6 on page 84.

In this interview, you'll learn more about the trials Chapman experienced while creating and launching the business and discover useful advice (based on her firsthand experience) about what it takes to make a startup Shopify-based business succeed on a tight budget.

FIGURE 5.6 Zoë Chapman designed the Kiddiwhizz website to sell her invention, the Whizzer.

Q: *What made you choose to design and sell your Whizzer invention?*

I have a background in product design and a degree in computer science, which is what I studied while attending university. I have always had a creative side and love designing in general. When I first invented the product, it was created for my son, who back then was a toddler. I was constantly on the go as a single mother, and he needed to go to the toilet often. I wanted a product that I could easily carry with me. Due to life in general, even after designing the product from scratch, I was not initially able to do anything with it until the COVID-19 lockdown happened and I finally had some extra time to focus on this project, which had been on my mind for so many years. My son just turned 9 years old.

I love learning new skills and the experience of testing new product designs. While the product was in development, I started learning about how Shopify operates by setting up an online store that I used to test the dropshipping business model for the products I chose to sell. Through this experience, I became aware of what the Shopify platform was capable of.

After having my original product design stolen, I had to redesign the product from scratch and learn how to protect every aspect of it legally by filing for appropriate patents, trademarks, and copyrights. When it came to selling my invention, I turned back to Shopify to create an ecommerce website that would support my business selling the Whizzer online.

Q: *What was the process of developing a Shopify website like?*

I took a Shopify theme and began customizing it. The greatest thing about Shopify is that anyone can take a theme and, without any programming knowledge, design a professional-looking website. I had a very specific look and website design in mind that I wanted for the product, so I found a theme that met those design and functionality needs. Using my design background and a friend's knowledge of programming, we then further customized the site by changing fonts, layout, and the design of the buttons, for example.

When creating graphical assets for the website, as well as my marketing materials and product packaging, I used Canva [https://www.canva.com/] to ensure that everything was consistent from a visual standpoint. I did not rush the website. I wanted to make sure it looked good when the company ultimately launched.

Leading up to that, I displayed a holding page that said the website was coming and invited people to share their email address so they could be notified when the Whizzer product launched. The holding page also invited people to follow the company's social media feeds for product updates. While the Shopify site consisted of just a branded holding page, I collected email addresses, which ultimately turned into a decent-size email marketing list that I used to promote the product's actual launch several months later.

Even before the Shopify site launched, I really engaged the customers by getting them involved with the product design and production journey. I would publish polls on social media asking for opinions about color options for the product's packaging, for example, so people felt like they were part of the whole product development and prelaunch process. I used Instagram as my company's primary social media presence initially, in part because Shopify integrates so nicely with Instagram.

Q: *For you personally, what was one of the biggest challenges when it came to launching your Shopify-based ecommerce site?*

It was putting together a system to handle all the order fulfillment and shipping. I did not have the money to hire a fulfillment company, so I needed to figure out how to handle this myself. To minimize the stress and time associated with order fulfillment and shipping, I used a UK-based service called Parcel2Go [https://www.parcel2go.com/], which is just like Easyship, ShipStation, or Shippo in the USA. It offers discounted shipping rates and great integration with Shopify.

Q: *What is the best piece of advice you can offer to a new Shopify-based ecommerce business operator?*

Shopify offers merchants a lot of data about traffic to their site and their customers. Study and then use this data whenever you're making relevant business, advertising, or marketing decisions. This data will show you where your site's visitors are coming from, how long they're staying on your website, and what they're doing while they're there. I recommend taking advantage of an abandoned shopping cart feature, which will automatically email visitors who start making a purchase but don't follow through. This gives you a second chance to earn the sale. Using analytics and the free tools offered by Shopify will save you a lot of time and provide a lot of valuable insight.

As someone is checking out and finalizing their purchase on your site, make sure you turn on the feature that encourages that customer to provide their email address to be kept up-to-date on their order's shipping details. Make the option state that the customer is automatically subscribing to your company's email marketing list unless they opt out, as opposed to vice versa. Then use an email marketing system to stay in touch with your customers and to help generate repeat business. Shopify offers powerful email marketing tools, but there are services that also allow you to create well-branded email marketing campaigns.

Q: *From the point where you came up with the idea for the Whizzer product to the time you launched your ecommerce website, approximately how much money did you invest into the business?*

I'd say about $30,000 U.S., which, compared to other startup companies that have done similar types of ventures, is very little. One way I saved money was that I did almost everything myself, from the product design to the website creation and the implementation of the company's marketing, PR, and advertising campaigns. I went into this with a good understanding of how Shopify worked, so I did not have to hire a lot of outside help. Anyone can create an ecommerce website hosted by Shopify, but that is not going to generate visitors to your site or sales.

Q: What are the most important skills someone should have when starting a Shopify-based ecommerce business?

You definitely need patience and persistence. Shopify gives you an amazing head start by providing the tools to design, manage, and launch an ecommerce website, but this is just part of the overall process of launching a successful online business. You really need to understand what Shopify offers and take advantage of the free learning tools that Shopify provides through its video tutorials and online forums.

Develop an understanding of what's going on behind the website and what you need to do to support the website. The little things you do to tweak your website using Shopify's tools will make a huge impact on your success. Invest the time you need to learn how the whole system works, and then think outside the box so your website and business stand out. In the first three seconds that someone visits your website, it must provide them with a compelling reason to stay. As soon as someone gets to your website, the two most important buttons they should see and have access to right away should be labeled "Buy" and "Learn More."

I actually have two versions of my website. One is for visitors accessing the site on their desktop computer and the other is formatted specifically for mobile devices. In the most user-friendly way possible, the primary goal of my site is to quickly transform a visitor into a paying customer. I understand that my website is an ever-evolving sales tool. I am constantly studying the analytics and looking for creative ways to improve the site in ways that'll appeal to my target customers.

Beyond those two buttons, if someone scrolls down on the website's home page, there's a snippet from every other section of the website so they can quickly get the gist of what the site offers and learn about the Whizzer product through a series of images and headlines. I use very little text to communicate a lot of information. For example, one of the first things people see on the home screen is a summary of customers' reviews.

Q: Many website design experts recommend that ecommerce websites should avoid using animated backgrounds and other flashy elements that could distract the visitor. Your website uses a very soothing and subtle animated background to your advantage. Can you explain this design choice?

I put a lot of thought into the color scheme and design elements used on the website and throughout all of my marketing materials. One of these design elements is a subtle wave in the background, which for the computer version of the website,

I chose to animate in a subtle way that's soothing to the eye and that generates a feeling of calm and relaxation. There is a reason behind every design and color choice I've incorporated into the site.

Q: *Beyond the core website page design tools offered by Shopify, have you taken advantage of any optional Shopify apps to add functionality to the site?*

I use the Omnisend [https://apps.shopify.com/omnisend] email marketing app, as well as apps from Google and Facebook integrated with the site. I also use Trustpilot Reviews [https://apps.shopify.com/trustpilot-reviews] for customer reviews, and the Parcel2Go shipping tool app [https://apps.shopify.com/parcel2go-1]. Since the Shopify theme I chose does not support hosting a blog that's connected to the site, I also use a blogging app.

I personally have stayed away from the current trend of using apps that add a pop-up game to the website because they irritate me, but I know that many people in my target audience, which is composed of parents, like these games that allow site visitors to win a product discount. I am thinking about adding this type of functionality in the future. When choosing apps, focus on how much they'll cost over time to use and what impact they'll have on the speed of your site.

My final piece of advice is for online merchants to download and install the Shopify mobile app onto their smartphone. It's available from the App Store for iPhones or Google Play Store for Androids, and it allows you to manage and oversee your business from literally anywhere. Plus, every time you receive a new order, you'll hear an audible alert. This alert makes me feel really happy and more motivated each time I hear it.

CHAPTER 6

Themes and Apps Help to Differentiate Your Website

Once you know what you'll be selling and who your target audience is and you've begun to visualize the layout and functionality you want for your website, you'll be in a much better position to choose an appropriate theme. Of course, once you adopt a theme, you can further customize it as needed.

In addition to the free themes Shopify offers, you can turn to independent website designers offering optional themes that provide the professional appearance and functionality your website needs.

Start by Browsing the Available Themes

The price of an optional theme runs anywhere from free to around $350. Start your quest for the perfect Shopify theme for your ecommerce website by browsing in the Shopify Themes store (https://themes.shopify.com), which is shown in Figure 6.1 on page 90.

To jump-start your search, start by clicking on the Collections pull-down menu near the top-left corner of the browser window. From there, you can narrow your search by viewing those themes that are best suited for a specific task. Menu themes include Works with Shopify Markets, Large Catalogs, Small Catalogs, Selling in Person, Selling Internationally, Minimalist Style, Trending This Week, and New Theme Releases.

Figure 6.2 on page 90 shows the initial screen that displays the results from the Trending This Week menu option. What's displayed here is updated hourly and is a selection of what other ecommerce business operators have recently chosen as the theme for their websites. Keep in mind that you want your website to stand out from your competition, so it's important to not choose a theme that resembles your direct competitors' sites.

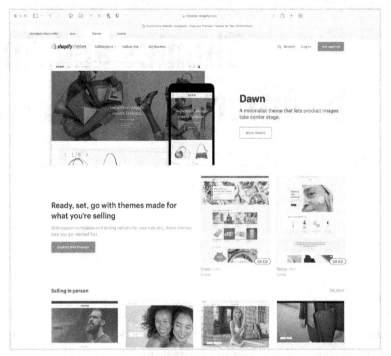

FIGURE 6.1 Choose from Shopify themes that allow you to choose the overall appearance of your ecommerce website. Each theme can then be further customized.

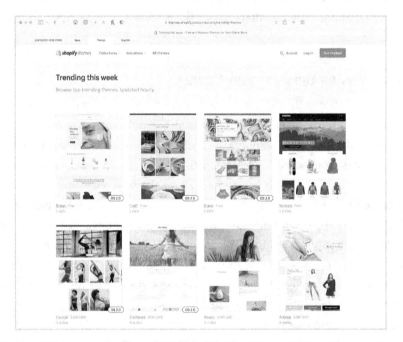

FIGURE 6.2 By clicking on the Trending This Week menu option, you can see a current list of the most popular themes available from the Shopify Themes store.

Displayed to the right of the Collections pull-down menu (also found near the top-left corner of the screen) is the Industries pull-down menu (shown in Figure 6.3 below). Clicking on this menu will bring up a selection of themes that cater to specific types of ecommerce businesses. Main menu options here include Art and Entertainment, Business Equipment and Supplies, Clothing and Accessories, Electronics, Food and Drink, Hardware and Automotive, Health and Beauty, Home and Garden, Pet Supplies, Sports and Recreation, and Toys and Games.

FIGURE 6.3 The Industries pull-down menu in the Shopify Themes store allows you to quickly find themes suitable for your ecommerce business, based on which industry it's in.

Choose the option that best fits what you'll be selling to see appropriate Shopify themes. In Figure 6.4 on page 92, the Home and Garden option was selected, returning 38 theme options. Keep in mind that you do not need to choose a layout from the category matching your business. You're free to go with any theme you wish, assuming it offers a layout and functionality that will appeal to your target audience and allow you to properly showcase what you'll be selling. Also, Shopify regularly adds more themes to each category, so you'll always have plenty of options to choose from.

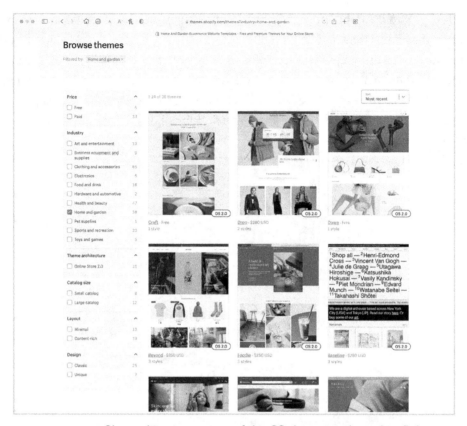

FIGURE 6.4 Shown here are some of the 38 theme options that fit in the Home and Garden category.

To view all the themes in the Shopify Themes store, click on the All Themes menu option near the top of the browser window, just left of center. After clicking on this option, you'll discover filters along the left margin of the browser window that allow you to narrow down your search using specific criteria, such as Price, Industry, Layout, and Design.

For additional help choosing a theme, you can click on the Search field near the top-right corner of the browser window and then type in a keyword, style, designer, or industry that is relevant to what you're looking for.

If you click on a theme, it is displayed in a separate web page. From here, you can see an overview of the theme's key features and selling points, in addition to its price and creator (shown in Figure 6.5 on page 93).

You'll notice two buttons located below each theme overview. One is labeled Try Theme and the other is View Demo Store. You can try out any theme for free and customize it however you want to determine if it'll meet your needs. You only pay for the theme if you decide to publish and use it.

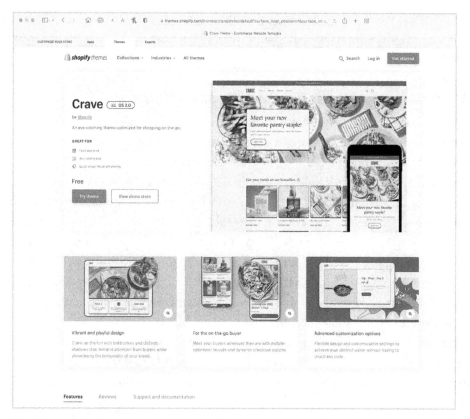

FIGURE 6.5 Read all the information pertaining to a theme before selecting it to ensure it'll meet your needs before you invest the time to customize it.

More important, click on the View Demo Store button to see a full-featured ecommerce website operating with the selected theme. This will give you a really good idea of what's possible using that theme and allow you to see how it looks and functions once it's fully populated with item listings and customized to fit a company's brand.

Continue scrolling down when viewing a theme listing to see additional clickable options, labeled Features, Reviews, Support and Documentation, and Customize with Apps. Click on the Features option to see screenshots of that theme, along with more details about what makes it unique. Click on Reviews to see ratings and reviews from other ecommerce business operators who have selected and used the theme. Support and Documentation gives you contact information about the theme's developer and allows you to download documentation regarding how it can be used and customized. Find out how to make your products stand out by clicking on Customize with Apps; you'll be shown popular apps that will help you add more features to your store.

Keep scrolling down, and you'll see a heading labeled More Themes Made for . . . . Here you'll see several additional themes from other developers that fit into the same category or pertain to the same type of business. Below those listings, there's a heading labeled More Themes by . . . , which lists additional themes created by the same developer as the one you're currently looking at.

Take Advantage of the Latest Theme Architecture and Standards

At the time this book was written, more and more themes were adopting the Online Store 2.0 design and architecture (a functionality Shopify added in July 2021), which takes advantage of additional tools, features, and functions provided by Shopify to offer a new standard in customizability and speed. As of early 2022, upgrading to an Online Store 2.0 theme was not mandatory, but for some ecommerce business operators, it was recommended for them to benefit from the added functionality. Ultimately, you might want to choose an Online Store 2.0 theme to stay current, regardless of what you'll be selling, assuming you can find a suitable theme for your specific business. In some cases, new versions of older ("vintage") themes have been created that comply with the Online Store 2.0 standards. When browsing themes, you can now select a filter to display only Online Store 2.0–compatible themes.

Because the speed of an ecommerce website is one determining factor in being able to hold a visitor's attention (and it helps to improve your SEO rankings), ensuring that your website runs as fast as possible will be to your advantage, and this is a major focus of the Online Store 2.0 upgrades.

According to Shopify (https://bit.ly/3NxlL60), some of the core upgrades to the Online Store 2.0 architecture include:

- Improved ability to customize the content on your online store's home page
- Greater capacity to add, rearrange, or remove sections and blocks within any website page to easily customize its layout
- Enhanced app support
- Capability to add richer content using dynamic sources
- Ability for customers to filter collections in your store (by things like price, availability, or color)

By the time you read this, Shopify Online Store 3.0 (or higher) may be available. Seriously consider selecting a theme that meets the latest standards so your ecommerce website will benefit from the upgraded functionality.

More Themes Are Available Elsewhere

Along with the themes that are featured in the Shopify Themes store, if you search Google or another search engine for "Shopify themes," you'll discover hundreds of independent websites selling additional Shopify themes. Some of these websites provide vast theme marketplaces, while others are from developers that have created just one or a small handful of Shopify themes.

Some of the independent theme marketplaces you might want to check out while seeking the ideal theme for your ecommerce website include:

- *Creative Market*: https://creativemarket.com/themes/shopify
- *Envato Market*: https://themeforest.net/category/ecommerce/shopify
- *Etsy*: https://www.etsy.com/market/shopify_themes
- *Out of the Sandbox*: https://outofthesandbox.com/collections/themes
- *TemplateMonster*: https://www.templatemonster.com/shopify-themes.php

Optional Apps Can Add More Functionality to Any Shopify Theme and Website

An app is an optional program that can be added to any Shopify theme or website to provide specific features and functions. The Shopify App Store (https://apps.shopify.com) has literally thousands of apps (also referred to as plug-ins) to choose from. Some are free, while others can be purchased outright or require an ongoing subscription fee to use.

The apps require no programming knowledge to add to your website, and incorporating the apps you select typically takes just a few minutes. Meanwhile, the apps you choose to add to your website can help you:

- Differentiate your website from the competition
- Better appeal to your target audience
- Provide special offers or incentives to your website's visitors
- Add interactive elements to your site to boost engagement
- Gather information from visitors to use later for marketing purposes
- Capitalize on current online shopping trends

However, the more apps you add, the slower your website will function. You also run the risk of confusing your visitors, cluttering up the site, or adding bells and whistles that just distract customers from your products.

Especially as a startup ecommerce website operator, it's very easy to keep adding apps to your site, only to discover the added features don't help your business or appeal to your target audience. Instead, carefully do your research and then only add one app at a time, so you can accurately measure the positive or negative impact it has on your business.

When you visit the Shopify App Store using your computer's web browser, located near the top-left corner of the page are two pull-down menus labeled Categories and Collections (see Figure 6.6 on page 96). You'll also see a Search field in the top-right corner.

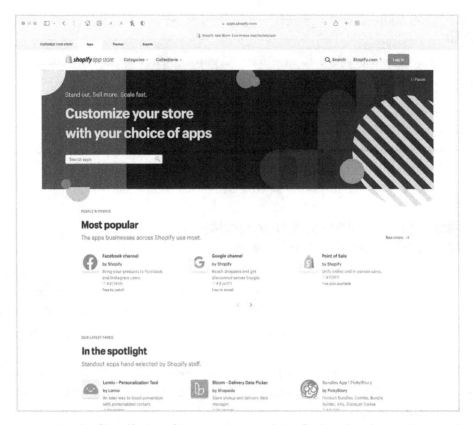

FIGURE 6.6 In the Shopify App Store, you can quickly find optional apps (or plug-ins) that'll add features and functionality to your ecommerce website, with no programming required.

Select the Categories menu option to narrow down your app search to a specific type of function. Your choices include Sourcing and Selling Products, Store Design, Merchandising, Marketing, Conversion, Fulfillment, Shipping and Delivery, Customer Service, and Store Management—all of which are areas you need to focus on as an ecommerce business operator.

The Collections pull-down menu allows you to sort and browse through available apps based on other criteria, including Launching Your Store, Growing Your Business, Works with Shopify POS [Point of Sale], Works with Shopify Marketing, Top Email Marketing Solutions, Made by Shopify, Sales Channels, Works with Shopify Checkout, and Works with Shopify Markets.

If you already know the name of the app you want, or you've determined the type of function you'd like to add to your website, go straight to the Search field and type a name, keyword, or search phrase based on what you're looking for.

Every app available from the App Store can be rated and reviewed by the website operators who use it, so pay attention to those reviews when choosing your apps.

Another important consideration is how each app will impact a website visitor's shopping experience. Some apps that benefit you use pop-up windows, which many shoppers hate. If you want a potential customer to tolerate an annoyance, you must make it worth their while, such as offering a 10 to 25 percent discount on their first order in exchange for their email address. The Spin to Win Popups app (https://apps.shopify.com/woohoo), shown in Figure 6.7 below, is an example of an app that collects email addresses, adds a sense of interactivity to a website, and offers visitors a discount on their order.

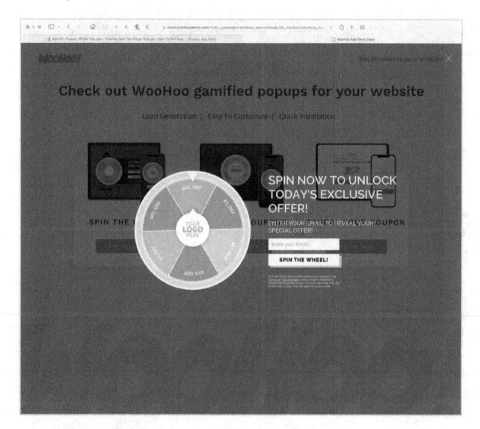

FIGURE 6.7 The Spin to Win Popups app is one of several that offer website visitors the chance to "win" a discount on their order in exchange for their email address, which the merchant can use in its email marketing campaigns.

Think carefully about what types of apps could benefit both you and your customers, and then make sure the added expense will be worthwhile.

Common Functions Merchants Add to Their Websites Using Apps

Once a customer adds an item to their shopping cart, several apps are available that will automatically recommend additional products the customer may find useful and potentially offer them a discount when they purchase a product bundle. They include Frequently Bought Together (https://apps.shopify.com/frequently-bought-together), Bundler–Product Bundles (https://apps.shopify.com/bundler-product-bundles), and Bundles Upsell | PickyStory (https://apps.shopify.com/product-kits-bundles-pickystory).

Depending on your target audience and what you'll be selling, you may find it extremely useful to be able to talk with your website visitors in real time via live chat or answer frequently asked questions using an automated chatbot. A bunch of apps are available to add this functionality to your website, such as Shopify Inbox (https://apps.shopify.com/inbox), Tidio–Live Chat & Chatbots (https://apps.shopify.com/tidio-chat), and HelpCenter | FAQ Chat Helpdesk (https://apps.shopify.com/helpcenter).

If you want to display reviews on your product listings to boost your company's credibility, especially with new customers, consider using an app such as Judge.me Product Reviews (https://bit.ly/3xfTVWW), Yotpo Product Reviews & Photos (https://bit.ly/3Mchowt), or Loox Product Reviews & Photos (https://apps.shopify.com/loox).

In 2021 and early 2022, one popular trend on ecommerce websites was the ability for customers to divide up the price of their purchase from a participating merchant into a series of interest-free monthly payments via a third-party service. Being able to pay through installments makes higher-priced items easier to afford for the customers, and for the merchants, it increases the chance of making a sale while still allowing them to be paid immediately.

The Affirm Pay-Over-Time Messaging app (https://apps.shopify.com/affirm), Klarna On-Site Messaging app (https://apps.shopify.com/klarna-on-site-messaging), and Afterpay Attract (https://apps.shopify.com/afterpay-attract) are among the apps that can easily add this functionality to your website.

Figure 6.8 on page 99 shows the demo store for the Klarna app. The black box on the right side of the browser window explains to the customer how their total purchase would be divided up into four interest-free payments. In this case, the Stealth Drone's full price is $229, so with Klarna, the customer would make four payments of $57.25 each. As the merchant, however, you'd be paid in full as soon as the online sale is finalized. For the merchant and for the customer, fees to use a service like Klarna may apply. Make sure you understand all the costs associated with using it before you opt to add it to your site as a payment/financing option.

As Shopify evolves as an ecommerce platform, so do its themes and apps, so when it comes time for you to figure out what features and functionality you want to incorporate into your website, look into what's possible, determine what your competition is doing, and then strive to offer an experience that your website's visitors and customers will truly appreciate.

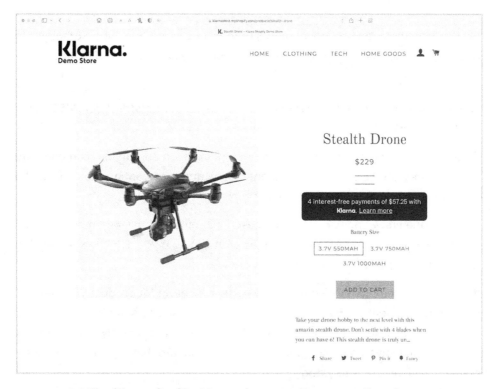

FIGURE 6.8 The Klarna On-Site Messaging app allows an online shopper to pay for their purchase from your website over several months, but you get paid in full immediately.

Sam Wright
Founder and Managing Director of Blink

The more experts you can learn from as you begin working on your ecommerce website, the better equipped you'll be to tackle any challenges you encounter and the more prepared you'll be to develop a website that'll help you achieve your business goals.

In this interview, you'll hear from Sam Wright, the founder and managing director of Blink (https://www.blinkseo.co.uk/), a UK-based SEO agency with a focus on data science. With more than 15 years of digital marketing experience, he and his firm have helped well-known global brands, including Rolex and Sotheby's, to prosper, as well as ecommerce small and midsize enterprises (SMEs) around the world.

Q: *What do ecommerce business operators need to understand about SEO and digital marketing?*

Over the past decade, what search engine optimization and digital marketing are and how they can be utilized has changed a lot, and they continue to evolve. The main principles, though, are still pretty simple.

For someone first launching a Shopify-based ecommerce business, making SEO a part of your overall strategy right from the start can help you achieve success, but it very much depends on your business.

It's really important to understand that Google isn't great for product discovery (at least at the moment)—SEO only works when you are selling something that either solves a problem they have or is something that they are actively looking for. At the same time, given how competitive many sectors are, having a point of differentiation with all this is key, too.

If you're selling a product that solves a particular pain point for your customers— and it aligns with what people are searching for—using SEO is absolutely the right way forward. If not, it's a case of deciding whether you can alter your product or positioning in line with this or choosing another marketing channel to focus on. Either is a valid approach, but each business will be different.

This is why before investing any money into SEO-related efforts, as an ecommerce business operator, you really need to understand your own brand and positioning before you can execute anything from a marketing point of view, because all your marketing efforts need to be focused on understanding your audience, knowing what keywords they'll be using, and understanding what types of problems and solutions they'll be searching for when surfing the internet or shopping online.

Once you understand this, you can build your strategies around those keywords and phrases within your marketing, advertising, and all the text that appears within your actual website, for example.

If you don't want to invest the time to learn how SEO strategies can be used, which can be as much of an art form as it is a skill set, hiring a digital marketing agency that specializes in this can help establish and grow your business.

Q: *If SEO comes down to knowing the right keywords or phrases to use, how can a startup ecommerce business operator discover the right terms to focus on?*

This is about understanding your positioning in detail. Everything stems from that, and it falls into the realm of doing your own market research and understanding who your target audience is and what it is about your company and products they'll find appealing. Once you start obtaining traffic to your website and converting them into customers, there are plenty of analytics tools that will help you discover how these people found you.

Q: *What would you say are the biggest misconceptions ecommerce business operators have about using SEO marketing strategies to enhance their business?*

I would say that they think SEO offers a quick solution to getting a lot of new sales. Instead, it should be part of your overall, long-term promotion, advertising, and marketing strategy and used to grow your business over time. If your website is underperforming or not achieving the success you hoped it would, this might be related to how you're utilizing SEO. It's more likely that you're not targeting the right audience based on the products you're selling. SEO marketing is a way to better reach your target audience, but you first must understand who that audience is composed of.

Q: *When people think about SEO strategies pertaining to their website, they think this means that the website must be listed as a first search result on Google or they're doing something wrong. Is having prominent search result placements on search engines necessary to achieve success?*

Getting a top ranking on a search engine does not necessarily translate into sales. Visibility is very different from sales. The goal of SEO is to have keywords or phrases that nicely match the intent of the buyer, so when someone searches for that phrase, the customer lands on your website and gets exactly what they want. Having lots of visibility on the search engine for lots of different keywords or phrases will not generate sales unless the keywords and phrases relate specifically to what you're selling and what the searcher is currently looking for.

Instead of focusing on driving a large and random crowd to your website, as a startup, I recommend focusing on a specific niche that's going to be less competitive, but where you'll have a more compelling offering than the competition. This is a more effective goal than just trying to gain lots of random traffic to your website or trying to achieve high rankings on the search engines.

Q: *How long should it take to see the benefits of good SEO marketing for a website?*

There are a lot of variables involved and no one answer applies to all ecommerce websites. Some will see results quickly, while others may not see any significant results for three, six, or even 12 months. A lot also depends on what SEO marketing strategies are used, the level of competition your company is facing, and the audience you're trying to reach. If you're looking for quick sales, I would recommend using paid advertising on social media services and Google. Where you should allocate your online advertising dollars should depend on your audience, their online habits, and current consumer trends.

Q: *What advice do you have when it comes to incorporating SEO strategies into product titles and descriptions?*

Put yourself in the mind of someone who would want to buy your product and then describe what the product is as accurately as you can. If there's a prescribed language that people would use to search for the product you're selling, this is the vocabulary you should be using. Also, when choosing categories and subcategories for your product, make sure you're very specific.

As you're composing product headlines and descriptions, it can be very dangerous to incorporate the same words or phrases repeatedly. Produce the best product headlines and descriptions you possibly can, knowing that if the right keywords or phrases appear within this copy once or twice, you'll be fine from an SEO standpoint. It's more important to make the headline and product descriptions as detailed and as high quality as possible. You could be penalized for using the same keywords repetitively. This is often referred to as "keyword cannibalism" or "keyword stuffing."

Also keep in mind that if there are ratings and reviews associated with your products, search engines like Google pay attention to that, in addition to what copy is related to your product listings. Google strives to drive its users to quality content that the user will be interested in, and when a product is involved, it's more apt to direct web surfers to what it determines are quality products, based on ratings, reviews, and the text-based copy associated with a product listing.

Q: *What's the best way for someone to learn about SEO marketing strategies for themselves?*

If you're a business owner, focus on the strategic stuff as a priority and really get to understand the types of things your target audience is looking for. Then learn how to use that information to your advantage by creating content that you know the audience will want to see. Getting bogged down in all the technicalities involved with SEO is like going down a rabbit hole. Understand the uniqueness of your products and then develop the content on your website around that.

As for the skill set, there are books you can read, classes you can take, Shopify apps you can utilize, and online tutorials that can help you understand the nuances of SEO marketing. There are plenty of tools out there, like Semrush [https://www.semrush.com], Ahrefs [https://ahrefs.com], Sitebulb [https://sitebulb.com], Clearscope [https://www.clearscope.io/], etc., that can be useful, but these are just tools—they don't replace strategic thinking.

In terms of how much it'll cost to hire an SEO specialist or SEO marketing agency, spending between $3,000 to $6,000 per month is probably average for a somewhat established ecommerce business, but this varies greatly. There are certainly highly skilled and experienced freelancers out there who will charge much less or much more than this per month, depending on your needs, their skill level, and the amount of work that needs to be done. It can help you understand the nuances of SEO marketing. One SEO tool we use in-house to help create content is Clearscope.

Like anything else, however, this is a skill set that takes time to learn and master. If you're in a hurry, hire an expert. Once you know you have a viable product to sell and you know your audience well, that's when hiring an SEO marketing specialist can begin to really help you.

Determine the Help You'll Need Before Hiring a Bunch of Experts

By now, you should understand that developing, launching, managing, and growing an online business will require you to use a wide range of knowledge and skills. If you lack a specific skill, it makes sense to hire the help you need in that area before you start making costly mistakes.

In Chapter 7, "Sources of Help," you'll learn more about the types of services and freelancers you can bring onboard to help you achieve your goals in the fastest and most cost-effective way possible.

Sources of Help

Unless you have the knowledge and experience to handle all the responsibilities associated with starting an ecommerce business, the most important advice in this book is that you should not try to do everything yourself (at least in the beginning). Just about every successful online business operator will tell you that if you hire freelancers and experts to assist with tasks you're not yet proficient at, you wind up saving yourself a lot of time and money. Plus, your business will start off with a stronger foundation.

Each chapter of this book focuses on a different phase of starting your business: creating, launching, managing, and promoting it. During each of these phases, take advantage of people with specific skill sets or areas of expertise to give yourself every possible advantage during the startup stage. If you have the time, you can always learn these skills yourself, but in some cases, you'll also need specialized equipment, and for those tasks, it's better to look for outside help.

Ways to Learn the Business Skills You'll Need

Whether it's accounting, bookkeeping, website design, writing, programming, graphic design, online advertising, social media marketing, SEO, customer service, photography, or videography, there are plenty of online and in-person classes available, as well as how-to books, to teach you these skills. The drawback is that it takes time to learn and master new skills, and just because you read and understood a book on, say, Facebook advertising, that doesn't mean you have the real-world experience to properly implement your newfound knowledge. You could still end up making costly and time-consuming mistakes.

If you need to acquire a skill to successfully operate your ecommerce business, consider taking free or low-cost adult education or continuing education classes, signing up for college classes, or finding online courses. Some online services that offer free or low-cost classes on various aspects of running a business include:

- *Coursera*: https://www.coursera.org/
- *Udemy*: https://www.udemy.com/
- *edX*: https://www.edx.org/
- *LinkedIn Learning*: https://learning.linkedin.com
- *MasterClass*: https://www.masterclass.com/
- *Shopify Learn*: https://www.shopify.com/learn
- *Skillshare*: https://www.skillshare.com/

You'll also find how-to information and tutorials, which tend to focus on teaching just one skill or cover one ecommerce-related concept, on these websites:

- *Business Advising*: https://www.pacificcommunityventures.org
- *Entrepreneur*: https://www.entrepreneur.com/events
- *SCORE*: https://www.score.org/
- *U.S. Small Business Administration*: https://www.sba.gov/

Pinpoint the Type of Help You Need

Chances are you won't need to hire all the different types of experts described in this section to help transform your business idea into a successful and profitable online venture. However, if you have the need (and the financial resources), any of the following experts will be able to provide you with valuable insights and help you save money, save time, and gain an advantage over your competition.

Accountant

An accountant will help set up your bookkeeping and accounting procedures, recommend how you should establish your company as a legal business entity, and help prepare your company's quarterly or annual tax returns for the IRS.

You'll typically wind up hiring an accounting firm (or CPA) to help advise you on taxes and prepare your tax return. Your accountant will not, however, be responsible for the day-to-day bookkeeping of your business. For this, you can use bookkeeping software or hire a part-time or freelance bookkeeper, depending on your needs.

The best way to find an accountant is through a referral from someone you know and trust. Alternatively, you can contact the American Institute of CPAs (https://bit.ly/3a7Twx1) for a referral.

Bookkeeper

A bookkeeper will be responsible for the day-to-day financial record keeping for your business. Ideally, you want to maintain your financial records with a widely used bookkeeping application designed for small businesses, such as Intuit's QuickBooks (https://quickbooks.intuit.com/accounting), Oracle's NetSuite (https://www.netsuite.com/), or Zoho (https://www.zoho.com/).

The person who handles your bookkeeping should be proficient at the application you have chosen and have a thorough understanding of every aspect of your company's finances, including accounts payable, accounts receivable, payroll, inventory, your bank balances, and all revenue generated by incoming orders.

Branding Specialist

This may be the same person who is responsible for your company's graphic design, content writing, and online advertising and marketing. Your branding specialist should be very familiar with your company's philosophy, story, products, and target audience. Their core responsibility is to help you make sure that every aspect of your Shopify store, marketing and advertising efforts, customer-service operations, and any other interactions you have with your potential and existing customers all use messaging and graphics that tell one cohesive story about your company that help distinguish it from your competition.

Your brand consists of your company name, logo, slogan, the fonts and color scheme you use online and in all printed materials, and your core messaging. Your branding specialist should help you define your company's brand and then ensure that it's properly used throughout all aspects of your business.

Keep in mind that your brand will likely evolve as your company grows, so it's a good idea to have your branding specialist review everything you're doing every few months and suggest ways to more clearly define and promote your brand.

Content Writer

This person will compose all the text that appears on your website, including your product descriptions. They may also be responsible for writing your product manual, blog posts, social media posts, email marketing campaigns, online advertising, press releases, product brochures, and any other text that you use to communicate with your existing and potential customers.

Your content writer should have proven writing, punctuation, and grammar skills, be fluent in the language(s) spoken by your target audience, and be extremely familiar with your company's brand, story, and products as well as your target audience (because just about everything they'll be writing must appeal to this audience).

Customer-Service Specialist

The customer-service specialist is responsible for creating your company's customer-service protocols and training every person who interacts with your prospects and customers to handle customer service in a uniform and professional manner that's consistent with your company's brand and philosophy. Whether you and your employees are communicating with customers and prospects in person or by email, live chat, text messaging, or telephone, the customer-service experience must be consistently top-notch.

Editor/Proofreader

Before you publish anything online or in print, you should have it edited and proofread by someone who understands your company's core messaging so that it's synergized with everything else your company is doing and contains absolutely no spelling or grammatical errors. The editor/proofreader should also make sure that it is written to appeal to your target audience and that it does not contain language that they will find confusing, misleading, or insulting.

Email Marketing Specialist

If you plan to use email marketing to solicit new business or generate repeat business from existing customers, it's essential that each outgoing email be well-written, perceived as informative and valuable by the recipient, properly targeted, concise, and able to use your company's core messaging effectively. Email marketing is a separate skill set from other types of online marketing. You must know how to use specialized software to compile and manage targeted email lists; compose nicely formatted, precisely worded emails; and then send out specific emails at proper intervals.

The person in charge of your company's email marketing must be proficient at using the email marketing software or service you choose and understand your company's email marketing goals. If you hire separate people to be your content writer, online advertising specialist, and/or branding specialist, it's essential that these people work well together.

Graphic Designer

When it comes to creating visual elements to represent your brand (including your company's logo) or artwork for your ecommerce website, typically a professional graphic designer or graphic artist will create this content.

Because graphic design requires artistic skill and training, most companies opt to hire this person on a freelance or per-project basis rather than trying to handle the task themselves. The graphic designer needs to understand your company, its philosophy, your target audience, and your brand, and be able to generate visually compelling content that'll appeal to your target audience (while taking your established brand into account).

While you can find a graphic designer or graphic artist through a referral, many websites, like Upwork (https://www.upwork.com/), allow you to browse through freelancers' portfolios and find people with the specific graphic design skills and experience that will meet your needs.

Lawyer

When it comes to establishing your company as a legal business entity with local, state, and federal governments; filing copyrights, trademarks, or patents for your business; composing any type of legal contract; facing a lawsuit against your company, or needing to file one against someone else—these are all services a lawyer can handle for you.

Over the long run, you'll want to establish a business relationship with an attorney you trust, so it's a good idea to get an initial referral from someone you know. However, you can also contact your state bar association or use LinkedIn to find a lawyer who specializes in ecommerce, copyright/trademarks, or business law, depending on your needs.

A law firm or individual attorney may require you to pay a retainer, but you'll need to negotiate an hourly fee you can afford. In some cases, an attorney will work on a flat-fee, per-project basis to handle tasks such as filing a trademark application on your behalf. If you opt instead to use a service such as LegalZoom (https://www.legalzoom.com/) to handle specific legal tasks, it will file legal paperwork or applications for you, but it typically does not offer legal advice or guidance.

Online Advertising Specialist

Your business can advertise online in many different ways, such as on other websites, via search engines, and through social media services. However, each advertising opportunity works differently. While all allow you to target a niche audience with your advertising message, the cost and reach of each service vary greatly, and understanding the nuances of how each one works will allow you to spend the least amount of money to reach the largest possible audience within your niche demographic.

Online advertising is both a skill and an art form, and it's constantly evolving as consumers' online buying habits change with new technologies that are introduced. Instead of taking a learn-as-you-go approach, which could result in costly mistakes, if you plan to spend a significant amount on online advertising, it's best (at least initially) to work with an online advertising specialist who understands your business, advertising budget, goals, and audience.

Let's say you decide to use Google Ads. When you contact Google, they will assign an advertising sales representative to help you. While this person undoubtedly knows the

Google platform very well, they do not know your business and will seldom invest the time needed to learn it.

You may discover their goal is to get you to spend as much money as possible on Google advertising, even if this is not necessarily the best fit for your business. Thus, it's best to work with an independent online advertising specialist who knows how to run successful campaigns on all the search engines, social media platforms, and website ad networks, and who will take a keen interest in helping you achieve your goals.

To this end, you'll need to pay the online advertising specialist their hourly, weekly, or monthly rate on top of the cost for each ad campaign. As the online ads begin to run, the specialist should help you understand the real-time analytics provided to you and help you fine-tune your messaging, reach, and spending to maximize your return.

You can find experienced online advertising specialists through Shopify Experts Marketplace, LinkedIn, or Upwork.

Photographer/Photo Editor

Featuring high-quality, high-resolution, clear, and detailed product images, along with lifestyle and brand photography, on your website is essential. Taking these professional-quality images is an art form, so if you don't have experience in this area, or if you don't own the necessary camera, lighting, and photography studio equipment, seriously consider hiring a professional freelance photographer to help you create this essential content for your website and online marketing campaigns.

Freelance photographers who specialize in product photography are listed on the Shopify Experts Marketplace, but you can also find them through Upwork and other freelancer websites. When negotiating with a photographer, try to agree upon a flat rate for the specific number and type of images you need (as opposed to an hourly rate), and make sure that the rate includes editing the images. You also want all rights for the images to be turned over to your company.

If you can't find a local photographer to work with, another option is to mail your products to a service that will photograph them for you. Of course, you can also invest in the lighting and studio equipment you need to create your own product photography, but the result must look extremely professional. When a potential customer sees out-of-focus, poorly lit, or otherwise amateurish images that don't showcase a product's details from multiple perspectives, they'll simply click away from your website, leaving with a negative impression of your products and your business.

Public Relations Specialist

One of the ways you can find new customers and drive traffic to your online store is to use public relations, as opposed to paid advertising, to get the media to review your products, interview your company's founders, or feature details about your business in newspapers, magazines, and other print media, as well as on the radio, on TV, in blogs, on podcasts, and on YouTube channels.

Like so many other things, public relations is both a skill and an art form that requires you to build positive relationships with media professionals—journalists, editors, producers, podcasters, YouTubers, etc.—so they'll include information about your company and its products in their editorial content. In addition to building these relationships, a PR specialist will compose and distribute press releases and full press kits for your company and its products and send out free product samples for review.

When you hire a freelance public relations professional or PR firm, they typically will require a minimum three-month commitment to create and manage a campaign that will generate media coverage for your business. Nonetheless, you should definitely consider using PR as an ongoing marketing and promotional tool.

Your best bet is to start by targeting social media influencers, podcasters, bloggers, and YouTubers who regularly create content that is relevant to your company's products. Choose people with large and well-established niche audiences, and get them to feature your products and company in their content. This is typically less expensive, easier, and in some cases more effective than reaching out to traditional media outlets like newspapers, magazines, radio stations, and TV shows. You can always do this yourself, but remember that PR specialists already have established relationships with media professionals and know how to create compelling and properly formatted press releases and press kits that cater to them.

SEO Marketing Specialist

Search engine optimization (SEO) and SEO marketing involves much more than getting your website listed as one of the top search results when someone types a specific keyword or phrase into a search engine such as Google, Yahoo, or Bing. SEO marketing involves using the right language (keywords, phrases, tags, etc.) on your website (and its code), in your social media content, and in all your other online content (blog posts, podcasts, videos, etc.) to make your products easier to find by someone looking for them online.

SEO marketing is constantly evolving, just like everything else on the internet. Sure, you could invest a lot of time and effort learning the nuances of how SEO works, or you could hire someone who has the experience and skill set already in place and use it to more effectively reach your target audience and generate more sales.

Your SEO marketing specialist may be the same person who handles your online advertising, as the skills and knowledge required to handle these tasks often overlap. You can find an SEO specialist through a site like LinkedIn or Upwork, as well as through the Shopify Experts Marketplace.

Keep in mind, not all the SEO marketing efforts you invest in will pay off right away. SEO marketing should instead be part of your company's long-term sales, marketing, and promotional strategy.

Shopify Store Creation/Setup Expert

Back in Chapter 5, "Creating Your Online Store," you learned the basics of using Shopify's store builder to design and create your online store using the theme you selected. One of the things that sets Shopify apart from other ecommerce turnkey solutions and platforms is that you can customize many aspects of the theme you choose to make your online store unique.

A professional Shopify store creation and setup expert understands the Shopify platform and has the programming and website design skills to transform a standard Shopify theme into a unique online storefront for your business by using much more than the drag-and-drop interface that Shopify provides.

Depending on what you're selling, your target audience, and your experience with ecommerce platforms, you may be able to use a Shopify theme and create a professional, functional online store on your own. However, if you want to incorporate more advanced features and functions that go beyond just adding a few apps, hiring an experienced Shopify store creation and setup expert can be beneficial, especially if you're looking to create and launch your website in a timely manner.

Depending on the type of work you need done, you may be able to negotiate a flat, per-project fee with this type of specialist, but most charge by the hour. Again, to find freelancers, check out the Shopify Experts Marketplace and services like Upwork and LinkedIn.

Social Media Marketing Expert

One of the primary ways to drive traffic to your online store is by using social media feeds on Facebook, Instagram, Twitter, TikTok, and/or Pinterest. Creating original, visually interesting, and highly engaging content that appeals to your target audience requires a significant time commitment and a strong level of creativity. And for this strategy to work, you need to post consistently over the long term, while engaging with your followers and subscribers on a more personal level.

While all sorts of tools exist to help you brainstorm and create awesome content for social media, if you don't have the time and wherewithal to do it yourself, consider hiring a freelance social media marketing expert to help you. Yes, social media marketing requires a significant time commitment. And if you pay someone to handle this task for you, it'll involve an added expense. However, it's also one of the most powerful and affordable marketing tools at your disposal, especially if you combine the content you post on your social media feeds with paid advertising on the platforms your target audience uses most frequently.

Your social media marketing expert may also manage your online advertising and SEO marketing. If you have different people handling these tasks, however, it's essential that they work in a cohesive fashion that integrates your company's brand and core messaging.

Videographer/Video Editor

Not every ecommerce website needs to use video (on the website itself or as part of its advertising or social media marketing strategy). However, using video clips on your website, on YouTube, in your online advertising, or in your social media posts allows you to convey more information about your company and its products in a fast and compelling way. If you choose to do this, however, it's essential that your videos look professionally produced, in 4K resolution with stereo sound, and that they're edited into concise clips that are informational and attention-grabbing.

Just as with photography, you can handle your videos yourself and do it all in-house (provided you have the right equipment and skill set), or you can hire a freelance videographer/video editor to create them for you.

Many online marketing companies specialize in video production, or you can hire an individual freelancer (or intern) to help you. If you're in a city that's also home to a college with a strong media arts or film/TV production program, finding skilled interns to work for little pay and in exchange for real-world experience and college credit will be easy and provide an excellent resource for your company. The Department of Labor website (https://www.dol.gov/agencies/whd/fact-sheets/71-flsa-internships) offers information about the legal implications of using paid vs. unpaid interns in a small business.

Videos that showcase a product's details and quality, compare your products with the competition, or demonstrate how to use your product can all add to your individual product listings on your website and be published on YouTube. Anytime you publish a new video on your company's branded YouTube channel, it becomes searchable on Google within minutes, providing a powerful way to drive more traffic to your online store. (We'll discuss YouTube more in Chapter 8, "Advertising and Promoting Your Products and Business.")

Showcasing professional-quality videos on your online store and/or YouTube channel can go a long way toward differentiating your company from the competition.

Website Designer

A website designer is typically someone with a graphic arts background who specializes in creating visually engaging websites that cater to a specific audience. A website designer may or may not have programming skills, but they are good at helping an online business develop and showcase its brand and ensure its website contains all the core elements and content needed to attract its desired audience and then convert website visitors into paying customers.

A website designer will help ensure your online store offers the features and functions that are needed without having any clutter and help you design a visually appealing website that provides an easy, effortless online shopping experience for your customers using the tools that Shopify (and optional apps) provides. A website designer is someone who knows how to program and create custom web pages, while a Shopify store expert may specialize more in customizing existing themes or templates.

Website Programmer

A website programmer or web developer is someone with programming knowledge who can fully customize the Shopify theme you pick for your online store. If you want to add unique functionality or fine-tune something in your store that can't easily be done with the available apps, hiring a freelance website programmer will be helpful.

This is not typically something you'll need to do right away, because Shopify's tools are straightforward and do not require programming knowledge to use. However, if you do need to go this route, try to build an ongoing relationship with a single programmer or web-development firm that specializes in Shopify. Each programmer has their own habits and ways of handling certain tasks, so if you're constantly switching developers, each new hire will need time to figure out the approach the last one used or will need to redo their work. This adds to the time and cost of customizing your online store.

Before hiring a programmer, make sure you can't accomplish your objectives with just the Shopify store builder, a theme, and one or more optional apps. Typically online stores that have unique needs (such as website features not offered by Shopify or a specific theme or plug-in) or that are expanding and require customized programming to address their customers' demands benefit most from hiring a website programmer.

Gather Your Dream Team

The people you opt to work with should all provide expertise, skills, and experience that you don't have yourself or that can save you a lot of time, thus allowing you to focus your own efforts on other responsibilities associated with the creation, operation, promotion, and growth of your business.

Whether you're hiring freelancers, interns, part-time employees, full-time employees, or even bringing on a business partner, the people you add to your team should have a proven skill set, experience, a belief in your company philosophy, and a willingness to adhere to your policies—and they should be people you mesh with on a professional level.

Be sure to learn as much as possible about each individual—their skill set, education, and experience—before hiring them. Ask to speak with past clients or employers, carefully evaluate their portfolio of past work (if applicable), and verify their credentials. Consider hiring them on a trial basis to handle one specific task. That way you can see if they're really a good fit for your company.

The Marketing and Promotion You Do Will Drive Traffic to Your Online Store

Whether you're using paid advertising, social media marketing, SEO marketing, public relations, traditional advertising, email marketing, YouTube videos, or other methods, when it comes to your company's advertising, marketing, and promotional efforts, adopt an ongoing and multifaceted approach that caters to your target audience's wants, needs, and media consumption/online habits.

The focus of Chapter 8, "Advertising and Promoting Your Products and Business," is to help you discover some of the many powerful options available to drive a steady flow of traffic to your online store. But first, check out this interview with David Wagoner, cofounder of full-service ecommerce agency P3 Media, whose only mission is to grow its clients' online businesses quickly and sustainably. In this interview, he shares his advice about ways to use the marketing tools available to ecommerce entrepreneurs to their utmost advantage.

To keep tabs on the most current ecommerce trends, you can subscribe to their free blog, *P3 Insights*, at https://pthreemedia.com/blogs/blog.

SHOPIFY EXPERT

David Wagoner
Cofounder of P3 Media

P3 Media (https://pthreemedia.com) applies its expertise with an integrated, data-centric lens that allows it to create best-in-class solutions for its merchants that are tailored to their unique needs. Using the company's experience, an online business operator should be able to raise sales and engagement. David Wagoner is the company's cofounder and chief marketing officer.

P3 Media's proprietary data-centric approach is enhanced with true hand-in-glove service. The company builds each new client relationship on a foundation of curiosity, empathy, and honesty. The people working at P3 make a point to learn each of its clients' businesses inside and out. Clients that come to P3 for individual projects decide to work with them again and again because P3's resources and philosophy allow them to go beyond merely building better web experiences to spec. When P3 partners with clients, it commits to developing an enduring, omnichannel roadmap that will help its clients achieve and sustain maximum revenue growth online.

Q: *P3 Media promotes itself as a Shopify Plus Partner. What does this mean for your clients?*

We are a highly vetted agency that works very closely with Shopify, on behalf of our clients, on new business initiatives and new integrations. About five years ago, we identified Shopify as what we believed to be the market leader in the space. Its platform provides elegant and customizable experiences for companies looking to sell products online. We decided to really focus our efforts on becoming experts on developing deep expertise on all aspects of Shopify and the surrounding ecosystem.

After identifying P3 Media as a firm that could execute complex jobs, Shopify added P3 Media to its small group of recommended Shopify Plus Partners. We don't just create pretty websites that use the Shopify platform. We use a data-driven design and development process to create high-converting web experiences that function exceptionally well and that evolve with the pace of technology to keep our clients ahead of their competition.

Q: *What advice can you offer to startups looking to launch a successful Shopify-based ecommerce site?*

Ecommerce is a 360-degree endeavor. But the first thing you as a business operator need to do is figure out what your key differentiator is and translate that advantage to your online experience. Do you onshore a hard-to-find product? Are you building a brand with a unique aesthetic? Have you created an innovative sales model or an environmentally conscious intervention in your space? These are all questions whose answers will direct effective web design. Shopify is a phenomenal platform for building in your differentiators because it's user-friendly and over-indexed on quality merchant solutions. Even without coding experience or a ton of startup capital, you can use their theme library and drag-and-drop design tools to dial in your message, and you can harness their deep native functionality or huge ecosystem of apps to create unique experiences that will help you stand out on your terms.

Initially, you'll probably be using a handful of freelancers to handle marketing, advertising, and website development or maintenance tasks for you. When it gets to the point where your business is profitable but you're spending a lot of time managing and juggling many different freelancers, that's when working with a digital marketing agency really makes sense. Once you've hit a revenue threshold of a few hundred thousand dollars a year, a full-service ecommerce firm like P3 Media can take your business to the next level with expert data-driven development and marketing services tailored to expand your business.

Q: *What features and functions of Shopify (and apps) should a startup ecommerce website be sure to take full advantage of?*

That's a really good question, but the full answer will vary based on what the company is selling, who they're selling to, the company's goals, and its budget. That said, if you're serious about growth, you'll need to use a number of tools right away: To keep your website compliant with accessibility laws, you'll need to implement a solution like AccessiBe [https://accessibe.com/]. To grow and harness your customer contacts, you'll need an on-site contact capture solution to feed your email marketing and SMS [short message service] platform. To capture goodwill and grow brand equity, you'll need to integrate a customer review solution. To maximize conversions, you'll need frictionless checkout options like Shop Pay, which allows both one-click checkout and dynamic checkout, and you'll need to add flexible payment options, like buy now pay later, which has become hugely popular among younger shoppers and can be implemented both natively and with third-party apps. If you're on Shopify Plus, you can go a step further and automate the majority of your order and fulfillment logistics using Shopify Flow.

Q: *What is the biggest misconception you've found that startup ecommerce business operators have about selling products online?*

People who don't yet fully understand ecommerce think that starting an ecommerce business and making it profitable is going to be easy. Many first-time online entrepreneurs think that just building a website is enough to make traffic start flowing to that website. People also tend to think that accumulating traffic is going to be inexpensive because it's possible, for instance, to go viral without spending a dime. But the truth is that it's incredibly rare to achieve that kind of breakthrough, and most companies that do are financing that breakthrough. There's a saying that goes, "When it comes to ecommerce, customer acquisition costs are the new rent." While you might not be paying rent for a physical office space, there are other expenses associated with advertising, marketing, and promoting your business that you'll incur to drive a steady flow of traffic.

Getting qualified traffic to your website costs money and takes time. Make sure you understand the amount of money and the level of energy that's involved in acquiring online customers. Making an early investment in customer acquisition is a step that's often skipped by up-and-coming online entrepreneurs. But we live in an attention economy, and companies of all sizes are fighting tooth and nail for the attention of potential customers in the online space. You need to be prepared to compete with a budget and a marketing plan that addresses all three levels of your customer acquisition funnel from Day One.

Q: *What are some of the most powerful marketing tools a startup ecommerce business should utilize?*

The most powerful marketing tool that a young ecommerce business can get is positive word-of-mouth advertising from its customers, but this has to be earned. You need to give all your customers a high level of focus and create the best possible experience shopping on your site. Customer interaction should feel personalized and attentive. For example, a handwritten and personalized note sent out with each of your orders will go a long way toward making your customers feel good about doing business with your company.

Once you're earning goodwill, it's essential to collect it via an on-site review system and to repackage your user reviews or user-generated content into organic and paid media efforts across your advertising channels. In descending order, online shoppers trust recommendations from their family members and close acquaintances, the influencers they follow, other customers, and then direct marketing from brands and businesses. In other words, you'll earn more sales more quickly by marketing with the voices of others than by trying to market solely with your own.

Developing partnerships with other companies that are trying to reach your same audience, but that are not competing with your company based on its product offerings, is another great, cost-efficient way to build your customer base. Once you find a suitable partner, you can do joint marketing and cross-promotions like loop giveaways or limited collaborations to drive traffic to both of your websites. This strategy requires more of a time investment, as opposed to a financial investment.

Q: *How important is a social media presence for online marketing?*

I believe it's essential for DTC [direct to consumer] ecommerce businesses to develop a strong social media presence in order to attract new customers and communicate with existing customers in a more informal way. Social media provides entrepreneurs with a cost-efficient way to create an organic and highly engaged community around a brand and its products. This is an important part of Shopify entrepreneurship. If you're able to build an audience of 50,000 to 100,000 or more followers or subscribers on social media, it becomes a really strong sales and marketing platform for your business. Building a strong organic following on a particular platform will amplify your paid media performance and improve your ROI. Plus, platforms like Instagram, Facebook, and even Twitter now have native shopping integrations with Shopify, so you can sell through your storefront directly on social and shorten the pathway to purchase considerably.

Q: *How important is developing a brand for an ecommerce business early on?*

While developing a brand is important, it's much more important for the online entrepreneur to have a strong and clear vision right from the start. I refer to a brand as a vision that's been packaged up for customers. Before coming up with a brand, you need to develop a clear understanding of what you want to build and what community you want to serve. Your company needs a purpose. Once you have a defined vision and purpose, that will manifest itself into a brand that you can then build upon for your customers. A company's vision and purpose need to be instilled within the DNA of its brand.

As an entrepreneur, you need to understand why what you're doing is meaningful, what story you want to tell, who you're trying to connect with, and how what you're doing is different from what's already in the market. Most of [the things] people buy online are not essentials. They are "wants." Consumers buy wants based on the story that's behind that product or service. They want to know if it's ethically sourced, made locally, who manufactures the product, and who the owner of the company is, for example. An entrepreneur with a clear understanding of their business's core value propositions and moated advantages can answer these questions in a way that enhances the value of the shopping experience for the customer, and that is the basis of durable brand building.

CHAPTER 8

Advertising and Promoting Your Products and Business

"If you build it, he will come" is a famous line from the 1989 movie *Field of Dreams*, which was about a farmer (played by Kevin Costner) building a baseball diamond in the middle of nowhere; at the end, people magically drive to see it, just because it's there. That type of magical thinking works great in Hollywood movies, but not in real life, especially when it comes to building and operating an ecommerce business using Shopify (or any other ecommerce platform, for that matter).

Creating a highly targeted website that looks amazing and offers only the very best products for sale is only a small part of the overall ecommerce equation for success. Once your site goes live to the public, it's your responsibility to aggressively advertise and promote it on an ongoing basis to drive a steady flow of traffic there.

At that point, it's a well-designed website's job to convert visitors into paying customers, which only a small percentage of the people who visit your site will become—no matter how targeted and prequalified they are. Realistically, a conversion rate of between 5 and 10 percent should be considered very favorable.

The moment you stop advertising and promoting your site (online and in the real world), the traffic will stop coming and your sales will dry up. It's that simple. Your best bet is to take a multifaceted approach to your advertising and marketing efforts. For the purposes of this book, *advertising* relates to promotional activity that you pay for, while *marketing* refers to promotional strategies that take time but don't necessarily cost a lot of money (or are free).

A multifaceted approach means that at any given time, you should be running at least three entirely different types of promotional campaigns designed to drive new traffic to your site. These campaigns can be any combination of the strategies outlined in this chapter (or anything else you determine could be viable), depending on what you're selling, your target audience, your available time, and your budget.

Some of the advertising and marketing campaigns outlined in this chapter require a significant financial investment (such as paid advertising), but once initiated, they don't take a lot of time to manage on an ongoing basis. Others, like becoming active on social media or starting a blog or a podcast, require a substantial time commitment but not a huge outlay of cash.

Keep in mind that it's also essential to provide a superior level of customer service to your customers, so you can turn website visitors into paying customers and existing customers into repeat customers. Then word-of-mouth (and their social media accounts) will also help promote your business. Always strive for an extremely positive, five-star review from every single customer, as many online shoppers pay careful attention to the ratings and reviews earned by the merchants they're buying from and the products they're thinking about purchasing.

This chapter focuses on a handful of popular techniques and strategies you can use to advertise and market your business in the most cost-effective and efficient ways possible. Regardless of which options you choose, remember to always focus your efforts toward reaching your target audience, and understand that you will need to commit time as well as money to the cause. When it comes to ecommerce, there are no shortcuts to success, and if you do succeed in attracting customers to your website, your competition will likely imitate you, so you'll have to switch things up every few months.

Also, once you decide on your strategy, make certain to continuously monitor the results and, when necessary, fine-tune your approach so you can spend less money (or time) to achieve better results. When using paid online advertising, you'll receive real-time analytics for each ad campaign you run, giving you insight into who is (or isn't) responding favorably to your ads.

10 Things to Consider When Planning Your Advertising and Marketing Efforts

As you embark on your advertising and marketing efforts, consider:

1. What the overall objective is
2. What audience you're trying to reach and why
3. What perceived value you're providing to your target audience (from their perspective)
4. What core messaging you're trying to convey
5. What results you're after
6. How much time you'll need to invest to achieve your goals

7. What the immediate and ongoing costs will be

8. Whether each individual strategy you adopt is working the way you hoped

9. How you can tweak your efforts to generate better results with a smaller time and financial commitment

10. What your competition is doing to attract new customers (and how you can do it more effectively)

Specialized Knowledge May Be Required

Each strategy in this chapter requires specific knowledge and a unique skill set. Of course, previous experience will also be helpful. You can invest the time to acquire the necessary knowledge and skills yourself or hire freelancers or independent contractors to assist you.

While hiring help will require an upfront expenditure, it will also help you avoid potentially costly and time-consuming mistakes, generate positive results faster, and allow you to focus more of your own time and efforts on tasks that you're good at and that will benefit your company.

Unfortunately, there's no guaranteed formula for success when it comes to advertising and marketing an online business. You'll need to understand the current ecommerce trends and the online shopping habits of your target audience, and then tap your own creativity to discover what combination of strategies works best for your business.

You'll also need to fully customize each advertising and marketing campaign so it caters specifically to your company's needs, nicely accommodates the products you're trying to sell, and allows you to efficiently reach your target audience with a message, story, and time-sensitive call to action they'll respond to favorably. Then adopt a well-thought-out implementation strategy that has realistic and measurable goals.

As a startup, even if you understand your product, brand, and audience perfectly, developing and implementing each advertising and marketing campaign will involve some trial and error. Expect to waste some time and money on things you thought were a great idea but that don't work out as planned. This is part of the learning curve.

However, by doing your research and seeking out the expert help you need to compensate for your lack of experience, knowledge, and skills, you should be able to minimize your losses and put more effort into the strategies that are clearly working in your favor.

Remember, except for paid online advertising, you should not expect instant results from most of your efforts. Some of these strategies will take days, weeks, or even months before you can accurately measure their effectiveness. Stay focused, be patient, do your research, and take an organized approach to your advertising and marketing efforts, while continuously monitoring the impact of each campaign separately.

Take Advantage of a Newsletter, Blog, or Podcast

Shopify provides a variety of optional tools, as well as apps, that make it easy to collect email addresses from visitors to your website, which you can then use for sales and marketing purposes, providing they opt into your mailing list.

Instead of bombarding potential and existing customers with an onslaught of sales emails (which can be bothersome to the recipients), consider creating and publishing a weekly, biweekly, or monthly digital newsletter, blog, or podcast that provides content your audience will perceive as valuable, insightful, and even entertaining.

Understand the Difference Between a Blog, Newsletter, and Podcast

A *blog* is a form of newsletter, but it's typically incorporated into the ecommerce website itself, anyone can access it for free, and it does not require a subscription.

For the purposes of this book, a *newsletter* is a digital publication that people can subscribe or opt into by providing their name and email address. You'll then email the newsletter to subscribers on a regular basis.

Both a blog and a newsletter use text, photos, graphics, and potentially audio and/or video clips to convey content to readers. A variety of blogging tools, as well as separate tools to compose, lay out, and distribute digital newsletters and manage subscriber lists, are available from Shopify and third parties.

A *podcast* is an episodic audio program (typically between five and 30 minutes in length) that you can produce and distribute via your own website and through podcast directories and podcast services, like Apple Podcasts, Google Podcasts, iHeart, Stitcher, TuneIn, Spotify, and Overcast. As with a blog or newsletter, ecommerce companies often use a podcast to attract new customers, informally communicate with their existing customers, and share content they believe their target audience will find useful.

Developing content for a podcast and then recording, editing, distributing, and promoting it is very inexpensive, but it is time-consuming. It also takes time to build an audience for a podcast, but once you do, that audience tends to be loyal. As of early 2022, podcasting is the fastest-growing media format in the world, while other types of media, such as newspapers, printed magazines, broadcast TV, as well as AM and FM radio, are on the decline.

Come Up with Creative Content on a Regular Basis

In your newsletter, blog, or podcast, some of your objectives might be to:

- Compare your products to the competition
- Delve deeper into your company's story and philosophy
- Introduce readers/listeners to yourself and your team members
- Share informative "how-to" content related to your products

- Explain how your products can be used to benefit the user in unexpected ways. Focus on how your products can meet the audience's needs and wants, provide a solution to a problem they're facing, enrich their life, or save them time or money.
- Preview new products you're about to launch on your website
- Promote special sales or incentives that are exclusive to your readers/listeners
- Discuss industry trends or major advances that directly relate to your products
- Answer questions from your audience about your company and its products

Consider Podcast Advertising Instead of Producing Your Own Podcast

If you like the idea of reaching podcast listeners but don't want to invest the time and effort in making your own podcast, another viable option is to pinpoint existing, successful podcasts that already target the audience you're trying to reach and then advertise on or sponsor those podcasts.

Many advertising services allow you to reach listeners by airing your ad across a wide range of podcasts, or you can reach out to specific podcast producers directly and offer to advertise on or sponsor those podcasts. The cost of advertising on or sponsoring a podcast varies greatly but is mainly based on the average size of their audience.

To achieve the best results from podcast advertising, commit to advertising on or sponsoring a podcast for at least 6 to 12 weeks (or episodes) before determining the campaign's effectiveness. Many podcast listeners will need to hear the same ad multiple times before they consider responding to it.

If you're interested in podcast advertising opportunities, some of the services you can use to get started include:

- *AudioGO*: https://www.audiogo.com/
- *Libsyn AdvertiseCast Marketplace*: https://www.advertisecast.com/
- *PodcastOne*: https://www.podcastone.com/podcast-advertising
- *Spotify Advertising*: https://ads.spotify.com/en-US/ad-experiences/podcast-ads
- *SXM Media*: https://www.sxmmedia.com/podcasts

Use Conversion Rate Optimization Techniques on Your Website

As you know, attracting a steady flow of traffic to your website is essential, but equally important is converting a portion of that traffic into paying customers. A variety of tools and optional Shopify apps can help you with this conversion rate optimization (CRO) task, using pop-up windows, follow-up emails, and other tools that kick in automatically if a visitor does something like abandon their shopping cart without finalizing a sale. However, there's a fine line between encouraging your visitors to respond to a call to action (i.e., click the Buy Button) and harassing them, so be careful about how you deploy these.

There are also apps and tools that, based on what items a customer puts in their shopping cart, will recommend related products for them to buy. If you're selling jewelry and someone chooses a necklace, these tools will automatically suggest the matching bracelet, ring, and earrings. Plus, as an incentive, you can offer a discount for purchasing multiple items.

Depending on your target audience, some of these tools can be extremely useful when it comes to boosting your conversion rate, but you need to proceed with caution so you don't wind up annoying, confusing, or harassing your website visitors.

If you decide to send abandoned shopping cart emails (which offer a reminder and added discount as an incentive to return and buy), that's great. But don't start sending versions of that email several times a day, every day, for the next week or two. This is a sure way to aggravate the recipient and get them to opt out of your email list, add your company to their spam filter, and start shopping elsewhere.

As for the apps that add flashy interactive gimmicks to your website that encourage visitors to buy more products, share their email address, or "win" an added discount on their purchase, these tools can be useful if used correctly. But you should know going in that most internet users hate pop-up windows and many have installed tools in their web browsers to block them. If you opt to use an app or Shopify function that generates pop-ups, use them sparingly, and make sure the benefit to your visitor outweighs the annoyance factor.

Also, by understanding the wants and needs of your target audience, you'll be able to better gauge in advance what gimmicks they'll appreciate and which ones they'll find annoying, hokey, confusing, or distracting. When it comes to soliciting names and email addresses from potential customers, offer them valuable incentives such as discounts. Never force them to share their information or try to trick them into providing it.

Email Marketing Will Keep You in Touch with Customers

First, there's a big difference between sending out spam (unsolicited emails) to thousands of unsuspecting people and sending out carefully worded and targeted emails to people who have voluntarily opted into your company's email list. Do not ever use spam as a marketing tool, as this will quickly tarnish your company's reputation.

Email marketing, on the other hand, is a powerful and effective tool, assuming the people you're sending the emails to have opted into your distribution list and the emails share content that the recipient perceives as useful, valuable, and informative (as opposed to just a strong sales message).

Many tools and services will help you compose, format, and distribute marketing emails and manage multiple email lists efficiently. If you use email marketing, you will see the best results by maintaining different targeted lists and including specific content of interest to the people on each list—such as prospective customers, existing customers, and loyal repeat customers. And always remember that managing your lists requires you to promptly remove the people from each list who opt out of it, and never harass people with too many emails too frequently.

15 Strategies for Managing an Email Marketing Campaign

When it comes to composing and managing an email marketing campaign, take these strategies into consideration:

1. Use a powerful and customizable email marketing tool (see below for some suggestions) to manage all aspects of your email marketing campaign and become proficient at using it before you start sending out emails.
2. Most email marketing services offer automation tools, which you should use to save yourself time.
3. Make sure each email you send out is personalized, relevant, and timely and caters specifically to the recipient.
4. The wording in the email's subject line is essential. It should be attention-grabbing and preview what the recipient can expect by reading the message.
5. Each email should be perceived as offering value to the recipient. Yes, offering a discount is worthwhile, but make sure the email also offers information they will find useful and valuable. Your goal is not just to sell products, but also to build a long-lasting and positive relationship with each recipient.
6. Do not focus on the hard sell. Keep things upbeat and casual. Use the emails to build an ongoing relationship with the people on your list.
7. Keep your emails brief and to the point. People have a very short attention span. If you don't have something important to say, don't send it.
8. Each email should include a clearly worded and easy-to-follow call to action and repeat it twice (including at the end of the message).
9. Proofread each email carefully to eliminate all spelling and grammatical errors.
10. Always be truthful. Do not create unrealistic expectations about your company or products.
11. Use email marketing to share your company's story and philosophy and to remind the reader how and why you do things differently or better than your competition. Make sure to focus on how this benefits the reader.
12. The formatting should be visually appealing. Use fonts, type sizes, and a color scheme that your target audience will relate to and be able to see clearly on whatever size screen they're using to read their emails.
13. If someone opts out of your email list, remove them immediately.
14. Be respectful of your subscribers. When they opt into your list, make it clear how often they can expect to receive messages from your company, and then stick to that

schedule. Never share your email list with other companies or online marketers, who might then harass your subscribers.

15. Before sending out a mass mailing to everyone on your list, be sure to test the message with a small and select group.

Every email or series of emails you send out to your list should have a specific, clear objective. It should also be consistent with your brand in terms of its appearance and messaging and encourage recipients to engage with you via email, text messaging, or social media. People want to feel like they're buying from other people, not faceless megacorporations.

Many of the email marketing services offer a variety of pricing plans. How much you'll pay per month or per year will depend on the size of your email lists, the number of users, whether you want your emails to link directly to product listings in your online store, and what other features and functions you need.

Take Advantage of Shopify's Own Email Marketing Tool

Shopify Email (https://www.shopify.com/email-marketing) allows you to get started for free—and send up to 10,000 emails per month. Just like the platform's store builder, it uses a template-based design system that requires no programming knowledge whatsoever.

You can design and compose branded email messages with ease and manage your email campaigns and mailing lists from within Shopify. This includes receiving real-time analytics in the form of text- and graphic-based reports that are easy to understand.

Once you use up your free 10,000 monthly email allocation, Shopify charges a flat rate of $1 per 1,000 additional emails (or 0.1 cents per email). There are no monthly or annual commitments.

Optional Email Marketing Applications

In addition to Shopify Email, numerous other cloud-based email marketing applications and services that can help you compose, format, and distribute emails, as well as manage email lists, also provide integration with Shopify. Figure 8.1 on page 129 shows a list of services that work with Shopify that you can use to create and manage an email marketing campaign.

Social Media and Influencer Marketing Are Extremely Powerful

When it comes to promoting your online business using social media, you have a lot of great options. Social media provides you with the opportunity to find new customers, reach out to existing customers, and build an online community around your company and brand.

Research your target audience and current social media trends, decide which social media platforms it makes the most sense to focus on, and then set up accounts for your

Email Marketing Service	Website URL	Price Range Per Month
ActiveCampaign	https://www.activecampaign.com/	$9–$259
Campaign Monitor	https://www.campaignmonitor.com/	$9–$149
Constant Contact	https://www.constantcontact.com/	$10–$45
HubSpot CRM	https://www.hubspot.com/	Starting at $45
Klaviyo	https://www.klaviyo.com/email-marketing	Based on number of contacts and whether you want text messaging capabilities, too
Mailchimp	https://mailchimp.com/email-marketing	Free–$299 (based mainly on number of contacts)
Sendinblue	https://www.sendinblue.com/	Free–$600 and up for more advanced needs

FIGURE 8.1 Candidates for Creating and Managing an
Email Marketing Campaign

business on those services. Whenever possible, use the same username for each social media service (as well as your website's domain name). Don't use your personal social media accounts as your primary business accounts.

Your company should have its own branded presence on all the various social media platforms, like Facebook, Instagram, Twitter, Pinterest, LinkedIn, TikTok, Snapchat, and potentially YouTube, but you should focus most of your time and energy on the platforms your target audience uses. Setting up and maintaining social media accounts is free, but to do it right requires a significant and ongoing time commitment, not to mention the creativity to continuously develop new and interesting content.

As you decide which social media services to focus on, also think about the best ways to use those services. On Facebook, you'd want to set up and maintain a branded Facebook page for your company (https://www.facebook.com/business). Then, once that page is set up and populated with some useful content that'll appeal to your target audience, you might want to take advantage of paid Facebook advertising to drive traffic to that page, as well as your ecommerce website.

Keep in mind that your Shopify-based store can integrate directly with Facebook and Instagram (https://www.shopify.com/facebook-instagram), so you can easily create and publish Facebook and/or Instagram ads and shoppable posts that link directly to your online store. The Meta for Business website (Meta is the parent company of Facebook and Instagram) offers free information and tutorials related to setting up a business account on those sites (https://www.facebook.com/business/help) and then using that content to drive traffic to your ecommerce website (or selling directly through your social media posts).

The goal of any company's social media account should be to build brand awareness, reach new customers, and engage with existing customers. This is easy and cost-effective on social media, especially Facebook, because you can identify, reach, and interact with a defined, niche audience.

Remember that although establishing your company's presence on social media is free, running highly targeted advertising campaigns on those platforms still costs money. On most services, however, you can create and launch an ad campaign for as little as $50.

Once you identify which social media services you want to focus the most on (based on your time, resources, budget, and which you believe your potential customers are most active on), follow any of these links to set up a free business account:

- *Facebook*: https://www.facebook.com/business
- *Instagram*: https://business.instagram.com
- *LinkedIn*: https://business.linkedin.com/marketing-solutions
- *Pinterest*: https://business.pinterest.com
- *Snapchat*: https://forbusiness.snapchat.com
- *TikTok*: https://www.tiktok.com/business/
- *Twitter*: https://business.twitter.com
- *YouTube*: https://support.google.com/youtube/answer/1646861

While the concept of maintaining a social media presence or advertising on social media is the same across all the platforms, each offers unique nuances that you'll need to understand to fully take advantage of each service when it comes to creating compelling and highly targeted content or ads.

Almost without exception, any online business that's targeting consumers should have a presence on social media. If you don't want to personally create content and engage with your followers, you can hire a social media marketer to do some or all of this work on your company's behalf. However, first make sure you define your goals, have clear messaging and a story you want to communicate, and know the target audience you're trying to reach. If you don't understand these elements, you can't expect a social media marketer to understand your company, its brand, its products, and your goals.

Likewise, advertising on social media (or selling directly on Facebook and/or Instagram) requires a totally different skill set and understanding of how each social media platform's advertising works. This is something you can learn—or hire experts to help you with—to ensure that every penny you invest in social media is spent properly.

21 Types of Content You Can Create and Share Using Social Media

On social media, you can use text, photos, graphics, animations, video clips, and/or audio to present your content in the most informative, attention-grabbing, entertaining, and engaging way possible. In fact, the ways your company can benefit from social media are limited only by your imagination, creativity, and how much time and effort you're willing to invest. Whatever you opt to share, however, it needs to look and sound professional.

While individuals can use social media to share their personal opinions on controversial topics like politics and religion, you should avoid these things when you're publishing on behalf of your company.

Instead, your company's social media accounts should focus on content that:

1. Promotes your products
2. Showcases your company's brand and philosophies
3. Compares your products with the competition's
4. Demonstrates what sets your products apart
5. Shows how to best use your products with how-to tips and information
6. Solicits and answers questions from potential and existing customers
7. Encourages your followers to discuss your company and products through your social media presence, where you can moderate it
8. Promotes upcoming new products
9. Encourages interaction by posting trivia questions related to your products and brand. (You can offer prizes, such as free products or product discounts, as incentives. However, make sure that anytime you host a contest online, it adheres to local, state, and federal laws and does not involve gambling.)
10. Offers online-only sales to your customers (specifically for your followers or subscribers)
11. Cross-promotes your products with other companies that target a similar audience but that are not in direct competition with your company
12. Shares relevant news stories that relate to your company and its products
13. Offers a behind-the-scenes look at your company and its products (such as how they're made). This might include a video tour or short interviews with your company's founders or product inventors.

14. Solicits feedback from your followers and subscribers about your website's approach, branding, product descriptions, product selections, photography, product quality, etc. If you ask for honest feedback from your loyal customers, you'll often receive it.

15. Allows you to sell individual products within each post (via integration with Shopify)

16. Focuses on providing a higher level of customer service and personalized interaction with your customers in an informal way

17. Introduces potential new customers to your company and what it offers, while providing value-added information and content for existing customers that allows you to strengthen your relationship and encourage repeat sales

18. Encourages your followers and subscribers to help you promote your business and products by asking them to share your posts and/or reviews of your products via their own social media feeds. In other words, you can use social media to help generate word-of-mouth advertising or encourage existing customers to post reviews of your products.

19. Uses appropriate and targeted SEO keywords and hashtags that make it easier for your target audience to find your social media content

20. Offers polls that allow people to vote on various questions. You can use their responses to figure out trends and pinpoint preferences among your followers and subscribers.

21. Uses photography or video clips to showcase your products being used in the real world by real people. This includes sharing content created and submitted by your customers, followers, and subscribers (with their permission).

Create a Social Media Plan and Content Publishing Schedule

Considering all the different types of content you could share on your company's social media feeds, it's a good strategy to plan your posts several weeks in advance and publish new content on a set schedule. This might include posting several times a day, once per week, or at specific times during any given month.

As you plan your social media calendar, focus on variety. Use different formats as much as possible, so your content is both contextually and visually compelling as well as timely, informative, and entertaining. For example, on Instagram you should publish traditional posts as well as Stories and Reels.

Whenever possible, try to work special holiday-themed content into your social media publishing schedule. Even less popular holidays or events can provide inspiration for specialized content that will appeal to your audience and offer a sense of timeliness. This website offers a comprehensive list of U.S. holidays you might be able to generate content around: https://www.timeanddate.com/holidays/us/.

When you're sitting down to plan social media content for the upcoming month, consider the 80-20 rule. This rule recommends that you use about 80 percent of your content to educate, entertain, and inform your followers and subscribers and the remaining 20 percent to promote your company, your brand, and your products. On your social media calendar, pinpoint the day and time each post will be published, and on which platform. Make sure you have the appropriate assets (photos, video clips, and artwork) created and/or gathered well in advance, and consider carefully what headlines, hashtags, keywords, and links you want to use in each post. Also make sure you proofread each post before publishing, post consistently, and track your results.

Throughout the month, keep a separate list of posts you want to create in the future, so you always have a selection of fresh ideas to rely on when it comes to developing new content. While you can write out your social media calendar on paper or create a spreadsheet, you can also find social media calendar templates online that you can download for free. Here are just a few of them:

- *Airtable*: https://www.airtable.com/templates/content-production
- *Asana*: https://asana.com/templates/for/marketing/social-media-calendar
- *Hootsuite*: https://blog.hootsuite.com/social-media-templates
- *Monday.com*: https://monday.com/lp/templates/store/marketing
- *Smartsheet*: https://www.smartsheet.com/content/social-media-plan-templates

Consider Using Influencer Marketing to Promote Your Business

Yet another way to use social media to your advantage is to pinpoint who the most powerful influencers are on each platform that caters to your target audience and then hire those people to promote your company and its products through their social media accounts, which may already have hundreds of thousands or even millions of loyal followers. This can be an expensive marketing option, but it's a way to reach a large and targeted audience quickly. While you can start out by partnering or sponsoring "micro influencers" (people with only a few thousand followers) for a very small investment, if you want to tap the marketing reach of the biggest influencers in your product category, you may need to shell out some serious money.

Many digital marketing agencies can help small businesses team up with social media influencers and develop advertising campaigns, product placement opportunities, and sponsorship opportunities with key influencers, some of whom may be teenagers with 10 to 20 million followers in your target audience.

If you can't afford to work with a digital marketing agency to match you with social media influencers, identify the influencers whom you'd most like to deal with and then check their online profiles for business-related contact information. Some influencers represent themselves, while others have managers or agents you'll need to go through.

To learn more about how you can use influencer marketing to promote your brand and products and drive traffic to your website, check out some of these online resources:

- *BEN: Be Entertainment*: https://ben.productplacement.com/influencer-marketing
- *Influencer Marketing Hub*: https://bit.ly/3NstP9a
- *Interdependence*: https://influencer.interdependence.com/im-1/
- *Shopify*: https://www.shopify.com/blog/influencer-marketing-statistics
- *Socialbakers*: https://www.socialbakers.com/platform/influencers
- *Sprout Social*: https://sproutsocial.com/insights/influencer-marketing
- *Upfluence*: https://get.upfluence.com

Harness the Power of Video on YouTube

YouTube is the world's largest collection of free, on-demand video content. Anyone can create, publish, and share videos by setting up a free YouTube channel. Companies can brand their YouTube channel and then have the service host video content that's showcased on their website or within their blogs or newsletters.

Yes, creating compelling videos is much more time-consuming (and potentially more expensive) than other forms of social media content. However, one 30- to 60-second video can communicate a lot of information (using live-action footage, animation, other types of graphics, captions, and audio). It's essential, however, that your videos are high-resolution (at least 1080 pixels), and that they look and sound professional.

One of the biggest benefits to YouTube is that each video you post becomes searchable on YouTube and Google within minutes. If you use SEO when creating your title, description, and tags, for each video you publish, you get one extra opportunity for someone to find your content during searches.

Google is the most popular search engine in the world, and YouTube comes in second. So if you publish 10 or 20 short videos about your company and its products on YouTube, that's many additional chances to appear in someone's search results when they're trying to find what you sell.

Within your videos and the descriptions, you can include links directly to your online store or specific product listings, so you can also use video content as a powerful sales and marketing tool. Using YouTube for business is very different from the way you use other social media platforms, but if you decide to try it, it can be a low-cost way to find and attract highly targeted visitors to your website, boost brand awareness, and enhance your company's credibility and online reputation.

Books such as *Ultimate Guide to YouTube for Business* (Second Edition) by Jason R. Rich (Entrepreneur Books) offer much more detailed information about how to use YouTube videos as a sales and marketing tool for your business.

SEO Marketing and Online Advertising Can Take on Many Forms

Most people think that search engine optimization (SEO) is just about earning a top search result listing on search engines like Google, Yahoo, or Bing when someone types in a keyword or phrase that relates to your company or products. There's also a common misconception that as an online business operator, your website must place at the top of search results to succeed.

But SEO marketing involves much more than that. If your online business is listed with the search engines, in most cases, top placement is not essential. Instead of spending a fortune to hire a company that will help you earn top placement, focus your money and resources on other aspects of SEO marketing that will be much more beneficial. When you create and publish a website, after a few weeks or months, it'll eventually get listed on the major search engines automatically. However, there are tools and services you can use to speed up this process. For example, Google's website (https://bit.ly/3I6uBq9) explains how to get a website indexed on this popular search engine.

For instance, in all the text that appears on your ecommerce website (and especially in your product descriptions and headlines), use SEO practices to incorporate keywords and search phrases. You also want to insert these keywords and phrases into the photo captions and metadata associated with the photography and graphics used throughout your website, as well as within all your online marketing and advertising.

Brainstorm and come up with a list of 15 to 20 keywords or phrases that relate directly to your company and to each product that someone would most likely use when searching for your company or product online. A variety of free online tools can help you seek out relevant keywords and search phrases that'll help you create and fine-tune this list, including:

- *Google Ads Keyword Planner*: https://ads.google.com/aw/keywordplanner/home
- *Google Trends*: https://trends.google.com/trends
- *KeywordSearch*: https://www.keywordsearch.com/
- *Semrush*: https://lp.semrush.com/ar_en.html
- *SE Ranking*: https://seranking.com
- *SpyFu*: https://www.spyfu.com/
- *WordStream*: https://www.wordstream.com/keywords
- *Wordtracker*: https://www.wordtracker.com/

Simply by incorporating a highly targeted list of relevant search phrases and keywords into *all* text related to your website, you will automatically benefit from many SEO practices. You may then opt to invest additional time and money to fine-tune your SEO strategies, either handling these tasks yourself or hiring an experienced digital marketing firm to help you.

Before we move on to the next section, let's note that any business can take advantage of SEO-related advertising on social media services to drive traffic to a website. But keyword-based advertising and/or search engine–based advertising such as Google Ads require their own knowledge base and skill set. Do your research and make sure you understand how each advertising opportunity works and what it costs, and then allocate an appropriate budget before you start spending money.

Take Advantage of Targeted Online Advertising

When it comes to using keyword or search-based advertising to find and attract highly targeted customers to your website in a cost-effective way, you have many options, including using search engines (and their affiliate networks) and social media advertising. Choose ads that will allow you to reach your targeted audience (based on their online habits) and that fit your budget.

Some online advertising opportunities worth exploring that could be used to quickly drive a steady flow of traffic to your website (for as long as an ad campaign runs) include:

- *Facebook Ads*: https://www.facebook.com/business/ads
- *Google Ads*: https://ads.google.com
- *Instagram Ads*: https://business.instagram.com/advertising
- *Microsoft Advertising*: https://about.ads.microsoft.com
- *TikTok Ads Manager*: https://www.business-tiktok.com/brand/
- *Twitter Ads*: https://business.twitter.com/en/advertising.html
- *Yahoo Native*: https://gemini.yahoo.com/advertiser/home
- *YouTube Advertising*: https://www.youtube.com/ads/

Directly through Shopify, you can run product-specific ads that link to your online store and sell products directly from Google and social media–based ads. For information about Google advertising and selling via Google Shopping using your Shopify account, visit https://www.shopify.com/google. To sell through Facebook and Instagram via your Shopify account, visit https://www.shopify.com/facebook-instagram. To handle TikTok advertising through your Shopify account, visit https://www.shopify.com/sell-on-tiktok.

You can also have your products listed and searchable through Walmart's website and on eBay when you're a Shopify seller. To learn more about this opportunity, visit https://www.shopify.com/walmart or https://www.shopify.com/ebay. Keep in mind that different fees apply when using your Shopify account to sell through Walmart or eBay, so make sure to build these fees into your profit margins when setting your prices.

The five biggest benefits to online advertising using search engines and/or social media are:

1. You can reach a very targeted audience (that you define).

2. The cost to launch and test paid advertising campaigns on each service typically starts around $50. If you spend any less, you won't be able to collect any meaningful data and the ad's impact will be minimal.

3. You can create and launch a campaign and start driving traffic to your website within hours—often less.

4. You're able to track the success of each ad and keyword or search term used in real time, thanks to free analytics tools.

5. You can simultaneously run as many different ad campaigns as you wish, and send online shoppers directly to your website's home page or to specific product pages.

Only Use Real-World Advertising If It's Niche-Oriented

While the audiences for mainstream media outlets, including TV, AM/FM radio, newspapers, and magazines, are on the decline, you still have opportunities to reach niche audiences through highly targeted media advertising.

If your online business focuses on selling golf-related products and accessories, it might make sense to advertise in a popular golf magazine, like *Golf Digest, Today's Golfer, Inside Golf,* or *Golf,* because you know the print and online editions of these publications reach your target audience.

However, if you're trying to reach a niche audience with your advertising, it rarely makes sense to advertise in a general-interest media outlet, such as a TV show, a radio station, or a newspaper, because you'll be paying to reach their entire audience, when only a small fraction might be interested in your product.

Cable television is one way to target very specialized niche audiences or very specific regions, which might make financial sense if you're willing to pay for the production and placement of a TV ad. If you want to advertise in mainstream media, do your research and determine which specific media outlets your target audience most frequently uses.

You'll typically find, however, that online advertising tends to be more highly targeted, more cost-effective, and more efficient at generating results than mainstream media advertising, unless your primary focus is on building brand awareness rather than immediate sales.

Word-of-Mouth Advertising Is Extremely Powerful

Without a doubt, one of the most powerful and cost-effective types of advertising your startup or small online business can and should capitalize on is positive word-of-mouth. In other words, persuading your customers to tell their friends about how wonderful your company and its products are.

Not only do people trust the opinions of their friends, family members, and co-workers, but they're more apt to immediately visit a website or try a product that comes highly recommended by those sources. As you'll see in Chapter 9, "Top-Notch Customer Service Is Essential," the easiest way to generate positive word-of-mouth is to provide everyone who visits your website with top-notch customer service and the most personalized shopping experience possible—even if a visitor does not immediately become a paying customer. These people can still tell others about your website and share details about your products on social media.

Another way to get your customers to help promote your products is to encourage them to write positive ratings and reviews for your website, as well as for various online services that publish consumer ratings and reviews. A number of optional Shopify apps will allow you to solicit, accept, and display customers' ratings and reviews. However, only do this if you're confident that most of these ratings and reviews will be extremely positive.

Trustpilot (https://marketing.trustpilot.com) offers an optional Shopify app with both a free and fee-based version that allows your business to collect and display customer reviews. Shopify also offers its own Product Reviews app for free (https://apps.shopify.com/product-reviews), or you can visit the Shopify App Store to find other apps that offer this functionality, including:

- *Ali Reviews*: https://apps.shopify.com/ali-reviews
- *Growave—Loyalty, Wishlist +3*: https://apps.shopify.com/growave
- *Judge.me Product Reviews*: https://apps.shopify.com/judgeme
- *Loox Product Reviews & Photos*: https://apps.shopify.com/loox
- *Stamped Product Reviews & UGC*: https://apps.shopify.com/product-reviews-addon
- *Yotpo Product Reviews & Photos*: https://apps.shopify.com/yotpo-social-reviews

Many of these services charge monthly or annual fees, and most of them do not allow online merchants to curate or edit the customer reviews in any way, so only use one of these apps if you believe you'll benefit from it. When your business can consistently display four- and five-star ratings with glowing reviews, it immediately boosts your credibility and reputation, especially among first-time visitors.

Reach Out to the Media Using PR Techniques

Public relations activities involve you developing relationships with reporters, editors, writers, producers, content creators, YouTubers, podcasters, bloggers, and other people who work in the media, with the goal of getting them to include details about you, your company, and/or your products in their editorial coverage. Obviously, for this to work, you need to target media outlets and journalists that cover topics related to your company and your products and that reach people in your target audience.

Reaching out to the media is typically done by sending a well-written, attention-grabbing, and properly formatted one- or two-page press release. In the press release, you want to tell a compelling story that will mesh with their editorial content. In a nutshell, explain who, what, where, when, and why, be timely, and be directly relevant to the media professional you're sending the release to. Accompany it with a cover letter, and potentially a full press kit.

A press kit includes detailed information about your company, its founders, and its products, as well as images and other more in-depth content, including recent press releases. If you're trying to get your products reviewed, you'll also want to send a free product sample to any working media professionals who request it.

Implementing a successful public relations campaign requires several important steps:

1. Develop a compelling story to tell, with appropriate messaging.
2. Compose a well-written and properly formatted press release.
3. Create a comprehensive list of media outlets you want to target and determine the most appropriate person to contact at each, based on what you're trying to accomplish. If you're trying to be interviewed as an expert in your field by a TV show, radio show, newspaper, magazine, or podcast, you'd typically want to reach out to the talent booker, producer, editor, or a specific reporter who covers your industry.
4. Send your press release with a cover letter to each person on your targeted list. You can do this via email or U.S. mail.
5. Wait a week or so and then follow up *once* with each recipient via phone call or email. Offer to send them a product sample and/or additional information or to set up an interview with a spokesperson from your company.
6. Publish all your press releases or media kit content (including detailed product images) on your website, under a menu option called Media or Press.
7. Without harassing members of the media, try to develop an ongoing relationship. Ideally, as your company makes new announcements or releases new products, the media professionals you have a history of working with will continue to provide free media coverage to your business.

When you use public relations, you do not have any control over whether a media outlet will cover your company, when that coverage will appear, or what that coverage will include. You can provide very specific messaging in your press releases and materials, but a journalist can write or say anything about your company and its products, especially if they're doing a product review.

However, when you can get the media to offer you free coverage, it helps attract new customers and visitors to your website, build brand awareness, and provide your company with additional credibility.

As you'll discover, developing and implementing a successful PR campaign requires its own unique skill set. It's also a time-consuming task that will cost some money to implement properly. If you're not familiar with the process, consider hiring a freelance PR professional or firm with established media relationships to help you.

If you choose to handle your own public relations efforts, you must first learn how to write a properly formatted press release and then develop a targeted media list to distribute it to. Many websites can explain how to write and format a press release, including:

- *Backlinko*: https://backlinko.com/write-a-press-release
- *Business Wire*: https://pr.businesswire.com/bw-create-press-releases
- *Cision PR Newswire*: https://prn.to/3GQBETj
- *JustReachOut*: https://blog.justreachout.io/how-to-write-press-release-for-product
- *Shopify Blog*: https://www.shopify.com/blog/how-to-write-a-press-release
- *Wix Blog*: https://bit.ly/3miwV3k

The following services sell customized and targeted media lists that you can use for your PR efforts, if you don't want to compile your own targeted list:

- *Agility PR Media Database*: https://agilitypr.com/media-database
- *Cision Connect*: https://www.cision.com/engagement/
- *EIN Presswire*: https://www.einpresswire.com/
- *Prowly*: https://prowly.com/magazine/best-media-database

You can also pay services to provide you with the names, titles, and contact information for media professionals, so you don't have to do this time-consuming research on your own. Plus, you can pay services to distribute your press releases electronically on your behalf; however, you'll typically achieve much better results if you reach out to media outlets on your own, unless you're using a PR professional who has established relationships with people in the media.

Keep in mind, PR is a long-term strategy, and you should set realistic expectations before you start. As the founder of a startup ecommerce business, you probably won't get booked on a national TV morning show or major radio station, or even have your story immediately picked up by a national magazine.

You'll have a much easier time reaching out to and getting coverage from smaller, local/regional, or niche-oriented media outlets, as well as from blogs, podcasts, and YouTube videos produced by influencers with large niche audiences. At least at first, this is a good way to allocate your PR resources.

Through research, you should be able to pinpoint the top 10 blogs, podcasts, and/or YouTube channels that might feature your company/products and reach your target audience. This is where you should start, as they're the most accessible media outlets, and they're always looking for new and interesting content to share.

Develop Cross-Promotions with Other Merchants and Companies

Yet another option for inexpensively promoting your ecommerce business is to team up with other small business operators who are trying to reach the same target audience but are not in direct competition with you. Then develop a cross-promotion that takes place on your respective websites, on social media, or in the real world. The trick to doing this successfully is to come up with cross-promotional efforts that are equally beneficial to both companies.

Become Active with a Charity You're Passionate About

If there's a nonprofit cause you're particularly passionate about, consider donating an ongoing portion of your profits to that charity and participating in any fundraising events it hosts. You could also donate some products to give away as prizes for fundraisers.

Being able to promote that your ecommerce business supports a charity gives you instant credibility among potential customers who also support that cause. Plus, when you participate in a charity's organized events (either as a sponsor or by donating products), your company will receive recognition from that charity that all its supporters will see and appreciate.

In terms of your company's brand, actively supporting a charity also helps establish your company's principles and humanize it, especially when you explain why your company has chosen to support this specific cause. (And remember: Your company's financial contributions to charity are tax-deductible.)

Marketing Tools Offered by Shopify

As we've already discussed, there are many positive reasons to use Shopify to create, publish, manage, and promote your ecommerce business. In fact, the Shopify website offers an entire section (https://www.shopify.com/market) that describes ways to market your business and showcases specific tools at your disposal. The articles and tutorials on the Shopify website are free, and many of the recommended tools are either provided free as well, or because you're a Shopify merchant you receive a discount if you use them.

Don't Forget About Shopify Apps

As you're designing and building your ecommerce website using the Shopify store builder, don't forget to visit the Shopify App Store and browse through the Marketing category (https://apps.shopify.com/browse/marketing). Here you'll discover more than 1,500 free or low-cost optional apps that you can incorporate into your website to add powerful marketing-related features and functions.

SHOPIFY EXPERT

Claudiu Cioba
Founder of VideoWise

VideoWise (https://www.videowise.com/) is a service you can integrate with your Shopify-based website that allows you to showcase what the company refers to as "shoppable videos," or videos that have an Add to Cart or Buy Now button embedded within the video content. The videos you're already producing for your social media feeds, like TikTok, Instagram, Vimeo, and YouTube, now directly sell your products, not just promote them.

Priced at $99 per month for its Starter plan or $399 per month for its Pro plan, VideoWise offers personalized advice on how your company should be using video and will show you proven results from leading Shopify brands when it comes to using VideoWise's best practices for increasing conversions using video.

The company's blog (https://www.videowise.com/blog) regularly publishes articles about how Shopify store operators can best use video content as a sales and marketing tool.

Claudiu Cioba is the founder of VideoWise, which evolved from a video-based product review company he also founded, called Reeview.app. He worked as a website and product designer for more than 15 years prior to launching his own business.

In this interview, you'll learn more about how to effectively use video as a powerful sales, marketing, and advertising tool using a five-star-rated Shopify app (https://apps.shopify.com/video-shopping) that ties directly into your Shopify-based ecommerce website.

Q: *What is a "shoppable video"?*

A shoppable video is an interactive video with an Add to Cart or Buy Now button on it that allows shoppers to purchase a product while watching the video. Conversion for shoppers who watch video is usually five times higher compared to the online store's average conversion rate. With VideoWise, you can turn any video into shoppable videos, and then display these on your Shopify store to boost conversions.

Q: *How does VideoWise increase conversions?*

Videos increase shopper engagement and make shoppers spend more time on your site. Shoppers will be better informed about your products and more inclined to purchase because of the unbeatable social proof that videos offer. We tested it and A/B tested it on more than 10 million online shoppers, and the conclusion was obvious. *If shoppers watch videos, they are more inclined to buy.*

Our studies with Shopify Plus stores have shown that shoppers who watch video have a conversion of up to 20 percent, compared to standard shoppers who don't watch video. *It's now a fact that video increases conversions, so the goal is to get more videos in front of your shoppers on your online store.* VideoWise is deeply integrated with Shopify, so the Add to Cart button within your videos and the checkout processes are handled by Shopify using your own checkout interface.

Q: *What are some of the ways a Shopify-based business can use videos on a product page?*

With VideoWise, you can add unlimited video widgets with as many videos as you want on the same individual web page or product page. For example, you can have one large presentation video on the top of your home page, a video or slide-based carousel in the middle that showcases video reviews from customers, and Instagram Stories on the bottom of the page for social proof.

Q: *What gave you the idea to start Reeview, which rebranded to become VideoWise?*

As an online shopper myself, every time I would set out to research something that I wanted to buy, I'd always go to YouTube and watch a series of unboxing videos related to that product. Unboxing videos provided me with a better view and presentation of that product, often from the point of view of other consumers. I began to wonder why all this video-based content was not being used directly by product sellers to help promote their products.

This curiosity led me to experiment with various ways to incorporate video content into ecommerce websites and pages designed to sell products. Around this time, Google released research showing that upward of 50 percent of online shoppers will leave a website that's selling a product to do online research before making that purchase. Since it's the goal of online merchants to keep their shoppers on their product pages, I really wanted to find innovative ways to use video as a tool not just to keep website visitors from leaving a website, but also to help convince them to make a purchase from that store.

At VideoWise, the goal is all about driving conversions using video content. We provide a no-coding solution for Shopify stores to do this easily and afford- ably. We use proprietary tools to help merchants find and display video-based content created by their customers. There is so much existing content on You- Tube, Instagram, and TikTok that merchants should be taking advantage of, but they don't even know it exists.

Q: *Should an ecommerce website replace text reviews and ratings with video reviews from customers on their site?*

No, the use of video should be in addition to the text-based reviews and product descriptions. The video content that's added to an ecommerce website should be complementary.

Q: *What advice do you have for producing or adding video content to a Shopify store?*

Businesses are reconsidering their position as video shopping explodes. To break through the competition, ecommerce stores will need to bring the dynamic ele- ments of offline shopping to online spaces. This means that creating and using video content is a must if you want to stay competitive in the new market. As Shop- ify stated, "Video is now the default expression of the internet"—it has become the main way this next generation of shoppers makes buying decisions. Consumers want to watch product videos before they buy—that's the new certainty.

Q: *What information should the "perfect" video product review from a customer include?*

The video review should include the reviewer's face. The person should also introduce themselves in the video and then be very transparent about how they use the product and their experience with it. The video should also show off the product and be less than two minutes long.

It's these video reviews that will generate the best conversion rate for the mer- chant. On average, a consumer will watch between one and two videos before making their final purchase decision, so a website does not need to include more than a handful of video-based reviews for each product to achieve good results.

Unlike video content you produce to promote your own products, customer video-based reviews do not need to offer superior production quality unless you're representing a very high-end brand. We have found that video-based reviews work for almost all product categories, but they work well when they're related to any type of tech or related gadgets, cosmetics, fitness, dietary supplements, pharmaceuticals, and home hardware. We have not seen as high conversion rates with video-based fashion-oriented reviews, however.

Choose Strategies That Are Appropriate for Your Business

This chapter outlined many different tools, resources, and strategies you can adopt when it comes to advertising and marketing your business. Not all these strategies, however, will work for every online business. You must determine (based on your target audience, objectives, and products) what will work best for your company, also considering your budget, time, and related resources.

To implement all the strategies we've discussed would likely require an entire marketing team working full time and would need people with some very specialized skills. To get started, pick just three strategies, and focus on using those strategies to achieve your objectives. You can expand your efforts as you increase your profits, gather more resources, and hire additional freelancers (or employees).

Start with the three advertising and marketing strategies that you believe will have the greatest impact, based on the money and time you're able to invest—keeping in mind that advertising and marketing are just two of your many ongoing responsibilities.

Finally, before you invest time and money into any advertising or marketing strategy, determine what your competitors are doing, and decide if your efforts will help lure customers away from your competition.

Even if you do everything correctly when it comes to setting up your Shopify store and launching your business, to make it sustainable, you'll need to continuously provide top-notch customer service to all your prospective and paying customers—without exception. What this means, and what'll be required from you, is explored in the next chapter.

CHAPTER 9

Top-Notch Customer Service Is Essential

By now, you should realize you need to deliver a handful of key components for success as an ecommerce business operator. One of the most important is to consistently provide the highest possible level of customer service.

According to research published by customer-service software company Help Scout, based on data from Microsoft (https://www.helpscout.com/blog/ecommerce-customer-service/), "There is a significant discrepancy in the perceptions of companies and buyers when it comes to the quality of service, as 80 percent of businesses believe they provide excellent customer service, but only 8 percent of customers agree."

Furthermore, 95 percent of online shoppers believe that customer service is essential to earn their brand loyalty, and Millennials are willing to pay up to 21 percent higher prices to do business with companies that provide superior customer service and make them feel respected.

Creating a superior customer experience (CX) includes everything you do to establish a warm, friendly, responsive, positive, and professional relationship with your website's visitors and customers, through every step of their interaction with your business. It should continue long after your customer receives their order.

Your customer-service efforts include how well and promptly you handle and resolve problems that would otherwise result in unhappy visitors and disgruntled customers, not to mention a higher level of product returns and refund requests.

Top-notch customer service means you're more likely to receive repeat business from customers, and they're far more likely to share positive information about your company through word-of-mouth.

You can implement a handful of strategies into your business practices to provide a positive customer-service experience for all your customers. Especially since the COVID-19 pandemic began and consumers began shopping online more frequently, they have demanded a higher level of customer service from ecommerce websites than ever before and prefer to do business with companies that show their appreciation to their customers.

This chapter focuses on developing and implementing effective customer-service practices and policies, as well as an overall customer-service plan for your ecommerce business.

Establish Your Customer-Service Policies and Practices

Your company's customer-service policies and practices should be well-thought-out, written down, and consistently observed. You might also want to include them in the About Us section of your website.

As with just about everything else related to running a successful ecommerce business, providing quality customer service means getting to know your customers and learning what they want, need, and expect from your business, and then exceeding those expectations while building a relationship with the customer that's based on mutual trust and respect.

It's a tall order, and if you hope to know your customers this well, you'll need to maintain detailed records using a CRM (customer relationship management) application. CRM apps allow you to maintain a database of your customers and their contact information, but they also allow you to document and track all interactions with each customer in one central place, so anyone working for your company can see their order history, past communications, and details of any problems they've had in the past (and how the situation was handled).

A CRM app puts customer-related information right at your fingertips, but it's not a magic bullet that solves your customer-service issues. It's just a tool you can use to create positive interactions with customers and prospective customers by quickly accessing and using pertinent information. Shopify provides basic CRM functionality, but you can also use a wide range of optional CRM apps, depending on your company's specific needs. These include:

- *Keap*: https://keap.com
- *Monday.com*: https://monday.com/lp/aw/crm-software
- *Salesforce*: https://www.salesforce.com/form/sem/customer-support/
- *Thryv*: https://www.thryv.com/
- *Zendesk*: https://www.zendesk.com/

Accessibility is another key component of customer service. Whether it's by telephone, email, text messaging, chat rooms, or social media, your prospective and existing customers want to know that they can easily reach an actual person at your company, not an AI chatbot or an automated email responder, and that their questions, problems, exchanges, returns, and refunds will be handled quickly.

While bots have their place in customer service for larger companies, for a small business—and especially a startup—interacting with your customers is essential, and you should build functionality into your website to provide it.

A good customer-service plan also means creating realistic expectations for your customers, and then exceeding those expectations. Personalized emails, handwritten thank-you notes, promptly returned phone calls, and maintaining a friendly and professional demeanor (even when your customers don't) are all vital components of a top-notch customer-service policy.

10 More Best Practices for Ecommerce Customer Service

As you're developing and documenting your company's customer-service policy, make sure to include the following strategies.

Strategy #1: Create Accurate and Detailed Product Listings

What you say in your product listings and how you say it goes a long way toward establishing a customer's expectations about the product. The quality and level of detail depicted in product photos (or videos) will also affect their perceptions of the product and the seller's credibility.

If you create expectations that are too high (by embellishing the truth or even lying outright), this will disappoint the customer when they receive their order and increase the odds of a return.

However, if your listings are accurate and create realistic expectations about a product you know is of high quality, the customer is more likely to be pleased when they receive the order and begin using the product.

Strategy #2: Display Your Order Return/Exchange Policy

Clearly display and share your company's product return and exchange policy—but be flexible. Although you can state on your website that you offer a 30-day, no-questions-asked return or exchange on your products, be willing to extend that deadline under extenuating circumstances.

If a customer contacts you on day 35 stating they've been sick, traveling, or dealing with a family emergency, tell them your company's policy but explain that you're willing to make a one-time exception to accommodate their needs. They'll appreciate your display of good-will and be more likely to return. Earning a repeat customer is worth making an exception, even if it means taking a financial loss on that sale.

Other policies you should share with customers on your website (during the checkout process, on your FAQ page, and perhaps elsewhere as well) include:

- Whether returns are accepted and what the return period is (7 days, 14 days, 30 days, or 45 days)
- The condition you require returned items to be in. Do you require the product to be unopened and in its original packaging, in resalable condition, with its original tags (or labels) attached, unused, unwashed, or unworn?
- How and when refunds will be issued
- What happens if the item is defective
- What happens if the item arrives damaged from shipping
- Who is responsible for paying the packing and shipping costs for returned items
- Where returned items should be sent, and what shipping service or method should be used. Will you be providing a return-shipping label? Will it be prepaid? Will the package be picked up by the shipping company, or will the customer need to drop it off at a local post office, UPS, or FedEx location or drop box?

Strategy #3: Display Your Company's Order Fulfillment and Shipping Policies

Feature your company's shipping options, costs, and policies on your website in an easy-to-understand and straightforward manner. Do not brag about your "Free Shipping!*" and in the fine print after the asterisk state that free shipping is only available on orders over a certain dollar amount. (It's fine to offer free shipping on orders over, say, $50—but make sure that fact is stated clearly and prominently, not in eight-point type at the bottom of the page.)

When it comes to order fulfillment, create realistic expectations in terms of order processing time and delivery time (based on the selected shipping method). If a customer pays extra for overnight shipping, they typically expect their order to be fulfilled and shipped that same day, so it arrives at their door the following day.

If you provide your customers with multiple shipping options at checkout, make sure you're clear about the added cost for premium or faster services, and be upfront about any delays caused by problems outside your control.

Using tools available from Shopify and third parties, follow up every order with a personalized order confirmation email (which can be generated automatically). As soon as an order is processed and fulfilled, send a second email with the package's shipping and tracking information, as well as its expected delivery date. Use this email as an opportunity to thank them for their patronage. A later email might encourage them to write a review of the product they ordered, or solicit feedback about their shopping experience. You can also mention any new or related products they might be interested in, although you should use a soft-sell approach for this.

Strategy #4: Stay in Touch with Customers and Show Gratitude

If a prospective or paying customer is willing to give you their email address, this does not give you an open invitation to send them multiple emails each day (or even every week). Be respectful and grateful for your customers. Every interaction you have with a customer should be personalized and include a written or verbal "thank you" for their patronage and support.

Strategy #5: Implement Live-Chat Functionality on Your Website

As of early 2022, a popular feature on ecommerce websites is a live-chat feature that allows visitors to enter a private chat room with a customer-service representative and get their questions answered or their concerns addressed.

The Shopify App Store offers multiple apps for incorporating a live-chat feature into your ecommerce website. You do not need to offer this feature 24/7 if you clearly post the days and times someone is available to chat. During other times, site visitors can leave a message that you can then respond to first thing the following business day.

Some optional apps that can add live-chat functionality to your site include:

- *Omega—Messenger & Live Chat*: https://apps.shopify.com/facebook-chat-1
- *Live Chat & AI Chatbot (Easy)*: https://apps.shopify.com/talkvisor
- *Live Chat, ChatBot, Cart Saver*: https://apps.shopify.com/chatra
- *Reamaze Live Chat & Helpdesk*: https://apps.shopify.com/reamaze
- *Tidio—Live Chat & Chatbots*: https://apps.shopify.com/tidio-chat

Strategy #6: Keep Things Simple When Communicating with Customers

Online shoppers want to be treated with respect and will choose to support online businesses that clearly strive to provide superior customer service. Some other quick and easy things you can do to promote this include:

- Prominently display your contact information throughout your website, making it clear that you and your team are available to provide support.
- Make your customer service available during the most extended hours possible, keeping time zone differences in mind and remembering that your customers will likely be doing their online shopping after work and on weekends.

- Your customer-service team should be empowered to help the customer (without needing to check with a supervisor) and have clear steps to follow so they can fix problems or address concerns immediately.
- Your customer-service team should never rely on prewritten scripts. They should be able to provide personalized service and solutions based on the customer's questions, problems, or concerns.
- Remember that a customer-service interaction is an opportunity to build goodwill and trust with the customer, not a chance to upsell them.
- Reward customers for being understanding. In addition to apologizing for a mistake or problem and taking immediate steps to fix it, offer an additional remedy, such as a generous discount on a future order, a refund of shipping charges, or a partial or full refund of their purchase price.

Strategy #7: Be Proactive in Addressing Problems

If you know in advance that there will be a delay in fulfilling an order—because the product is back-ordered, the shipper is taking longer to deliver packages than usual, or some other issue—tell your website's visitors about it *before* they place their order and follow up with customers to keep them informed about what's happening with their order and when they can expect delivery.

Always apologize for your mistakes and take responsibility for providing a timely remedy that the customer accepts as fair. But before you suggest a solution, listen carefully to the customer and make sure you understand their problem or complaint.

Strategy #8: Use Social Media as a Customer-Service Tool

Your company's Facebook Page, product-oriented Facebook Groups, or your online presence on any other social media platform can be used to communicate with customers informally and provide customer service. However, remember that social media is designed to be a public forum.

Even if you're using direct messaging or private messaging, social media is probably not the best venue for dealing with complaints, problems, or refund/return requests. If a customer reaches out to you over social media with a problem, try to switch the conversation over to email or a phone call, to prevent the conversation from taking place publicly on social media.

Try to dissuade customers from posting a negative review about your company or its products or bad-mouthing your company on social media. This content is much more apt to go viral (and be remembered by others). One way to stop this is to make direct contact with the disgruntled customer and come up with a way to make them happy. Perhaps offer to refund their money or send a replacement product at your expense.

Strategy #9: Use a FAQ to Provide Self-Service Answers

Publishing a FAQ (frequently asked questions) on your website that answers the most common customer service questions your website visitors and customers ask is *not* a comprehensive customer-service solution.

Some customers prefer to look up answers to their questions themselves and get quick answers, but most online shoppers want to talk to someone from your company when a question, concern, or problem arises.

Thus, you should definitely provide a detailed FAQ outlining your company's policies, particularly relating to returns, refunds, guarantees, and warranties, but you should also offer a variety of direct communication options for website visitors so they can receive personalized help and answers when they need them.

Strategy #10: Solicit Feedback from Customers

You can use a variety of tools to solicit your customers' feedback about their online shopping experience, such as customer-satisfaction surveys or direct email. Pay careful attention to the responses—especially when you see common trends start to emerge.

A customer-satisfaction survey should take no more than five minutes to complete. In exchange for completing the survey, offer your customers a discount on a future order or some other incentive they'll perceive as valuable.

In addition to asking a series of multiple-choice questions or questions that ask them to rate something on a scale from 1 to 10, conclude the survey with at least one optional, open-ended question that allows the respondent to write out a full response, sharing a compliment, suggestion, idea, or criticism.

Many apps are available to create and distribute customer-satisfaction surveys, and some integrate directly with Shopify. Some of these include:

- *AskNicely*: https://www.asknicely.com/customer-feedback
- *Delighted*: https://delighted.com/product
- *Enquire Post-Purchase Surveys*: https://apps.shopify.com/enquire
- *Reputation*: https://reputation.com/products/surveys
- *SurveyMonkey*: https://www.surveymonkey.com/
- *Zigpoll Customer Surveys*: https://apps.shopify.com/zigpoll

In addition to using your customer-satisfaction surveys to improve your overall business, you can use the feedback to generate ideas for new products and discover ways to outperform your competition. If you simply ask nicely, customers who have had a good experience with your company will be happy to provide you with helpful and honest feedback, while customers who have had a less pleasant experience will give you an opportunity to fix problems and avoid similar situations in the future.

SHOPIFY EXPERT

Andrew "Maff" Maffettone
Founder and CEO of BlueTuskr

Throughout this book, a lot of emphasis has been placed on hiring experts who can help you handle tasks associated with the setup and management of your ecommerce business that you don't yet have the skill set or experience to handle yourself.

Andrew Maffettone is the founder and CEO of BlueTuskr (https://www.bluetuskr.com/), a full-service digital marketing agency that's a Shopify Partner. It focuses on working with ecommerce sellers to handle their content marketing, search engine marketing, social media marketing, web design and development, marketplace marketing, and omnichannel marketing. Maff himself has worked in ecommerce for more than 15 years, and in this interview he shares some valuable advice based on his experience. A Shopify Partner is a company that has built a relationship with Shopify and that meets its guidelines for offering products/services to Shopify store operators.

Q: *How did you get started working in ecommerce?*

I have been involved with digital marketing for more than 15 years, but about eight years ago pivoted to focus exclusively on ecommerce. When I launched my own agency, it made sense to become a Shopify Partner and to focus on working with Shopify-based business operators because of the popularity and flexibility of the platform.

BlueTuskr solely focuses on the digital marketing aspect of running a Shopify business, and we pride ourselves on knowing and understanding the Shopify App Store and being able to suggest specific apps for our clients to utilize within their sites to achieve the best results. Some of our clients come to us for a custom Shopify-based website design if they don't want to customize one of the existing themes, or they'll come to us for help coming up with conversion optimization tactics that utilize optional apps. We also help our clients drive traffic to their sites using all aspects of digital marketing.

Q: *What would you say are the core skills someone should have when starting an ecommerce-based business?*

If you're just starting off, you really don't want to take shortcuts creating your website. You need to have a website that's fast, well-branded, and clean and then focus on how you'll be driving a steady flow of targeted traffic to the site. When choosing your Shopify theme, make sure you choose one that offers the functionality you need, but that will also entice your target customer. We see a lot of startup businesses choosing any random theme, thinking that they all work the same way and that they're basically interchangeable, and this is not the case.

Organizational skills are essential. When developing a website, you need to take a well-thought-out and organized approach, and then you need to handle every other task in an organized manner. If details start falling through the cracks and smaller tasks don't get done correctly, the whole business is going to suffer. An unorganized Shopify store becomes very hard to scale moving forward.

Q: *What tips do you have for developing a company's brand?*

If you're just starting out, you probably have very little hard data about who your target customer actually is. It's more about considering who you want your target audience to be. In the beginning, use a survey and market research service, like SurveyMonkey [https://www.surveymonkey.com/market-research/], to do some data-driven market research and determine who really is your target customer.

Until you have an accurate customer profile, you can't really build a brand that'll be intriguing to that audience, and you should not yet be making decisions about your logo, color schemes, product packaging, and marketing plans, for example. Once you know your target audience and start developing your company's brand, make sure that the brand is consistent across your entire website and everything else your company does online and in the real world, including what you do on social media.

Once your store goes live, use the data and analytics to make sure you're actually targeting the right people with your website and marketing efforts. In the beginning, you need to be flexible and adjust your efforts accordingly as you learn more and more about the people who are actually visiting your website.

Q: *What are some of the biggest mistakes you see startup ecommerce businesses making?*

The most common thing is that people think they can choose a random Shopify theme, throw up some product listings, create some posts on social media, and that will be enough to immediately generate sales. It's not that easy. You need to put some effort into your business, build a community, and entice people to visit your website.

When you're first starting out, you need to figure out where your potential customers congregate online and start building a presence there. You do not need a presence on every social media service. Once you understand your target customer's online habits, you can build an online community based on the social media platform they most frequent, while keeping in mind that social media habits and trends change regularly, so you'll need to adapt accordingly over time.

You may discover that your target customers spend more of their time listening to podcasts than they spend on social media—in which case, it might make more sense to either start your own podcast or start advertising on the podcasts your target audience is already listening to. Figure out what the best ways are for you to communicate with your potential customers and start there.

Another mistake I see Shopify merchants making early on is that they install a bunch of Shopify apps to add a lot of additional functionality. Adding on too many apps, however, can slow your site down and often provide for features you don't actually want or need. If you just need one specific feature, it might make more sense to hire a programmer to create and implement that one feature to your site, as opposed to adding an app that could slow down your site and offer functionality you don't ever plan to utilize.

Be very selective when choosing which of the thousands of Shopify apps you incorporate into your website. Over time, let the data show you where you might need help and what features or functions from an app would be beneficial. There are many apps that offer overlapping functionality, so do your due diligence, research your app options, and then compare their features, ratings, and pricing to find the best fit for your business.

Q: *Right from the start, are there specific app functions that a Shopify-based ecommerce site should use?*

I am a strong believer in displaying customer ratings and reviews, so an app that allows you to collect and then showcase this information is definitely worthwhile. If you want to incorporate pop-ups into your site, I am a fan of Privy [https://apps.shopify.com/privy]. I also highly recommend incorporating an email marketing system into your website. My recommendation for this is to use Klaviyo [https://apps.shopify.com/klaviyo-email-marketing].

If you're selling higher-priced products, a successful trend right now is offering a buy now, pay later option to your customers, using a service like Affirm [https://apps.shopify.com/affirm]. It only makes sense to offer this, however, if your average order is $150 or more. These services tend to work very well, and many sellers are seeing an almost instant uptick in their conversion rate when they start offering this type of financing option.

Q: *As a startup, how can an ecommerce entrepreneur calculate an accurate marketing and advertising budget when composing their business plan?*

Even if you don't initially have the budget to hire a digital marketing agency, consider hiring a freelance digital marketing expert to analyze your goals and recommend an initial marketing and advertising plan that's realistic and that will help achieve your initial goals in the most efficient way possible. Find someone who knows the ins and outs of digital marketing, so based on your target audience and startup capital, they can make informed recommendations and help you define an initial marketing and advertising budget that makes sense.

From a digital marketing expert, you want a customized list of things you could do to launch your company and drive targeted traffic to your site, as well as recommendations about how much you should spend within a specific time frame to achieve the desired results.

For example, if the expert recommends running social media ads, and the average cost per click on Facebook is $1.20, and the average conversion rate in your industry is 2 percent, you'll know that if you spend a specific dollar amount on Facebook ads, what you can expect from that campaign. In the beginning, your ad conversion rate might be very low, but with tweaking, you should be able to get it up to between 4 and 6 percent.

For a startup, becoming active on social media is usually the most cost-effective way to go when it comes to creating and sharing content, building an organic online community, and using targeted advertising to build your customer base. Once you decide which social media services you want to build a presence on, develop an understanding of the best practices for that specific service.

The approach you should take will differ between Facebook, Instagram, Twitter, and TikTok. I always recommend that you start on one service, become good at using it, and then expand to another service without spreading your resources too thin. Hiring a social media marketing expert on a short-term basis will allow you to learn from what they're doing, and then you can decide whether this is something you want to handle yourself or continue paying someone else to handle for you.

Don't spread your resources too thin, especially if you have a lower budget. If you're selling many different products, launch an online marketing and advertising campaign for your bestselling product and focus just on that initially. Once those campaigns are successful on an ongoing basis, expand and create additional campaigns for other products.

Q: *How important is providing top-notch customer service, and in your opinion, what does this entail?*

Providing a superior customer-service experience is essential. I am a big fan of incorporating a live-chat feature to ecommerce websites so customers can get even their most basic questions answered quickly and in a personalized way. Even if you hire someone from overseas who speaks fluent English to monitor your website's chat feature during off-hours, you'll likely discover that having this customer-service feature will improve your conversion rate. The key is to have a human responding to the live-chat feature and to not use an AI bot.

Another key customer-service strategy is to make it very easy for your customers to contact you directly, via telephone, email, text message, social media, or a live-chat feature. Do not make a potential customer jump through hoops to contact you. Also make sure all your company policies for returns, product exchanges, guarantees, and warranties are clearly displayed and easy for customers to find.

I am a big advocate of incorporating a blog into an ecommerce website as a customer-service and marketing tool, but the blog has to be structured correctly and kept up-to-date with content that readers will perceive as being valuable and informative. Blogs should provide extra content to help the customer but should never allow or encourage the visitor to click away from a product page, where they might buy something, in favor of reading an article.

CHAPTER 10

Fulfilling Your Orders

Five basic categories of things can be sold via an ecommerce website. These include:

1. *Tangible Products.* Tangibles are any products you'll be selling and shipping directly to your customers with inventory you'll maintain. This includes products you create or manufacture.

2. *Downloadable Items.* Ebooks, audiobooks, videos (downloaded or streamed), electronic publications, NFTs, digital artwork (including photography), computer games, apps, and any other items that can be purchased online and then immediately downloaded by the customer.

3. *Items That Will Be Dropshipped by a Third Party.* These are tangible items that your ecommerce website promotes and sells, but the inventory is manufactured and/or maintained by a third-party dropshipping company that will fulfill (ship out) the orders on your behalf to your customers. Order-fulfillment companies will also warehouse your inventory and process incoming orders on your behalf for a fee.

4. *Print-on-Demand Products Created by a Third Party.* These are tangible products that you promote and sell via your website, but they will only be created once you have an order by a third-party company, which will then ship the products to your customers.

5. *Services.* This includes any type of service that is sold online but is then performed virtually or in the real world. For example, hiring a plumber or landscaper online and then having humans come to the customer's home to perform the work.

As an online business operator, if you're selling downloadables, you need to ensure your website makes it simple for customers to purchase and download their desired products. Shopify offers the tools needed to sell and distribute downloadable products directly through an ecommerce website.

If you'll be working with a dropshipper or print-on-demand company, you must find reputable and responsible businesses that offer high-quality products, maintain an adequate level of inventory (so your customers don't have problems with sold-out or back-ordered products), and fulfill orders in a timely and reliable manner. Shopify also has integrated tools for selling products from dropshippers that are partnered with it.

Visit https://www.shopify.com/dropshipping to learn more about the dropshipping business model. Meanwhile, you can find more than 100 million different products to sell via dropshipping through the Oberlo app (https://www.oberlo.com).

When selling services online, you must not just persuade people to purchase those services, but also ensure the work gets done as efficiently, professionally, and quickly as you promised it would.

Fulfilling Your Own Orders for Tangible Products

If you're selling tangible products and plan to fulfill your own orders (the primary focus of this book), you have an additional set of responsibilities. First, you have to acquire and maintain ample inventory for every product you sell, and then you need to handle your own order fulfillment.

This requires you to develop relationships and accounts with shipping services and maintain a shipping department from your business location. You'll also need to allocate time in your daily schedule to package and ship all new orders as they come in and arrange for the orders to be picked up or dropped off with the appropriate shipping services.

Part of your shipping operation should involve creating a fun, exciting, and memorable unboxing experience for your customers once their order arrives. The Fulfillment Lab (https://www.thefulfillmentlab.com/ebook/how-to-create-an-unboxing-experience) offers a free ebook for online business operators that explains how to use unboxing to enhance your customers' shopping experience, differentiate your business, and improve your brand recognition. You may also want to use branded shipping materials, such as boxes, shipping labels, or tissue paper, that display your company's logo and use its color scheme.

Shopify Shipping (https://www.shopify.com/shipping) is a collection of tools for your website that automates some of the tasks associated with fulfilling orders. When a new order comes in, Shopify Shipping will create a packing slip, customer receipt, and shipping labels; adjust your inventory levels; and send emails to customers confirming the order and then notifying them when it's been shipped and giving them the package's tracking number.

But even with these helpful tools at your disposal, you must still physically package up the orders, prepare them for shipping, and get them to the appropriate shipping service—and that will take some time.

Establish Your Own Shipping Department

Once you determine exactly what you'll be selling, you'll need to figure out the best, most economical, and safest way to ship those items to your customers and then maintain an ample supply of shipping materials so you can quickly prepare orders for shipping.

The packing and shipping items you'll need will depend on what you're selling and how you'll be shipping them, but will likely include:

- Shipping boxes
- Packing tape
- Styrofoam peanuts or Bubble Wrap
- Shipping labels
- Thank-you cards
- Packing slips and customer receipts imprinted with your company name and logo

Initially, you may only need to ship out a small number of packages per day or per week, so you can purchase your supplies at a local office-supply superstore, such as Staples or Office Depot. However, as your business grows, you can save money by purchasing your shipping supplies in bulk and having them delivered right to your (home) office. A few popular wholesale shipping-supply companies include:

- *Amazon Business*: https://amzn.to/3xkxIHf
- *eSupplyStore.com*: https://www.esupplystore.com/
- *PackagingSupplies.com*: https://www.packagingsupplies.com/
- *The Packaging Wholesalers*: https://www.packagingwholesalers.com/
- *Uline*: https://www.uline.com/cls_shipping

Set aside an area in your home or office for your "shipping department." Here you'll want access to a wireless printer and (ideally) a separate shipping label and postage printer, all your shipping supplies, a package/postage scale, and a large table. For ease, set up your shipping area close to where you're storing your inventory.

Either through Shopify Shipping or another company that works in conjunction with your Shopify-based website, set up an account that allows you to generate prepaid shipping labels for USPS, UPS, FedEx, DHL, or whichever shipping services you plan to use.

Many services, like ShipStation (https://info.shipstation.com/print-shipping-labels), Shippo (https://goshippo.com), or Stamps.com (https://www.stamps.com/), offer discounts with the major shipping companies, and some even provide free shipping labels and other supplies. Which service you should choose will depend on:

- What you're shipping (weight and dimensions)
- Shipping volume (the number of packages you'll be shipping per day or per week)
- Insurance and delivery-speed options
- Pricing
- Company's reputation
- What shipping services (USPS, UPS, FedEx, etc.) are offered
- Ability to track packages
- Integration options with Shopify
- Package pickup or drop-off requirements (and daily cutoff time)
- International shipping options (if applicable)
- What shipping supplies (if any) are offered for free
- Customer-service availability

Once you've chosen the shipping service you'll use to prepare packages to be sent via one of the shipping companies, purchase a label printer that can generate compatible shipping labels for that service. A stand-alone, wireless thermal shipping label printer will cost between $100 and $300, depending on the size and manufacturer. The shipping service you choose will recommend an appropriate and compatible shipping label printer.

Based on your shipping needs and how many packages per day, week, or month you'll be shipping, it might make sense to establish accounts directly with one or more of these shipping services in order to get the lowest rates possible:

- *DHL*: https://www.dhl.com/us-en/home/dhl-for-business.html
- *FedEx*: https://www.fedex.com/en-us/ecommerce/shipping-options.html
- *UPS*: https://www.ups.com/us/en/business-solutions/business-shipping-tools.page
- *USPS.com*: https://www.usps.com/business/

Ideally, whichever shipping options you choose, they should integrate directly with your Shopify-based website as well as with whatever tools you're using to manage your inventory and bookkeeping.

10 Tips for Keeping Shipping Costs Under Control

As an unfortunate side effect of the COVID-19 pandemic, shipping costs have skyrocketed, and all sorts of shipping delays and problems have become commonplace. This will likely continue for a long time after the pandemic is officially under control, and you'll need to account for it financially and logistically when setting up and managing your ecommerce business.

Shopify's website offers a free Shipping Carrier Statuses page that is continuously updated with information about shipping issues. Access this information at https://bit.ly/3I201yb.

To help keep shipping costs under control, whether you plan to offer free shipping and cover these costs or pass along the charges to your customers, here are 10 strategies to consider:

1. Try to reduce the size and weight of packages.
2. Select the right size box for what you're shipping.
3. Take advantage of flat-rate shipping (with package tracking and insurance), such as USPS Priority Mail, when possible.
4. Use discounts offered by Shopify Shipping or other shipping services.
5. Based on your shipping volume, negotiate rates directly with shipping services.
6. Make sure all outgoing packages are trackable and properly insured.
7. Automate as much of the shipping process as possible to reduce time spent fulfilling orders.
8. Regularly check with the various shipping companies to track rate increases and seek out lower rates from competitors.
9. Avoid adding a separate "handling" charge to fulfill orders. Instead, build the cost of shipping supplies and "handling" into your product pricing and pass along exact shipping charges to your customers if you do not opt to offer free shipping.
10. If the shipping company charges for package pickups, deliver your outgoing orders directly to their nearest office or package drop-off location.

Another unfortunate responsibility of your shipping department will be handling product returns and exchanges. Create an efficient system for handling these tasks so that once a product has been returned, you can process a quick refund to your customer or promptly ship out a replacement item if an exchange is necessary.

In addition to having a set process for handling these tasks, properly document each transaction in your inventory and bookkeeping system (either manually or automatically).

From a business operations standpoint, you want the inventory management and order fulfillment process to be as streamlined, automated, and cost-effective as possible, while still being able to meet or exceed your customers' expectations by providing fast and reliable order processing. Amazon has set a high bar for online shoppers, who now expect online orders to be processed the same day and delivered within a few business days. Unless there is something unusual about your products, your customers will expect similar service.

Develop an Order-Fulfillment Routine

The speed and efficiency with which you process and ship your orders directly correlate with the quality of customer service your company is perceived to offer. Once you know the latest possible pickup or drop-off time for packages with the shipping service(s) you'll be using and determine how much time it takes to process and ship each order, schedule your order fulfillment and shipping early enough in the day to make sure new orders are shipped the same business day whenever possible.

Many ecommerce business operators will start processing their orders every weekday at 3 p.m. and then drop them off or arrange for a package pickup by 5 p.m., but this schedule will depend on your location and the shipping services you'll be using. Develop a daily routine that allocates ample time to handle order fulfillment but also gives you time to juggle all the other tasks you'll need to handle. If necessary, hire someone to help with your order fulfillment to ensure orders get shipped out in a very timely manner.

The Shopify Fulfillment Network Is Another Option for Order Processing and Shipping

Instead of managing your own inventory and fulfilling your own orders, Shopify offers an optional order fulfillment service for qualified products within the United States, where you ship your inventory to one of Shopify's warehouses, and then, for a fee, Shopify handles order fulfillment and shipping for your company. A Shopify-based business must apply to use the Shopify Fulfillment Network and must ship a minimum of three orders per day. Products sold can't be regulated or perishable. To learn more about this service, visit https://help.shopify.com/en/manual/shipping/shopify-fulfillment-network.

Other independent services will also handle order fulfillment, but depending on your profit margins, the additional fees may make these services too expensive to use. If you do choose to use one, Shopify offers tools that allow you to integrate an order fulfillment service directly with your website, so information on incoming orders is automatically sent to the service to be processed and shipped.

SHOPIFY EXPERT

Jeri Wambeek
Cofounder of WAOConnect

As you have seen, one of the ongoing challenges ecommerce business operators face is managing inventory efficiently. Jeri Wambeek is an inventory management specialist, author of *Stock Control Success,* and cofounder of WAOConnect (https://www.waoconnect.com/), a company in New South Wales, Australia, that specializes in cloud-based inventory management mainly for multimillion-dollar businesses. The insights she shares, however, can be applied to virtually any business that manages its own inventory, including startup ecommerce companies.

Q: *Tell me a little about your background and the services that WAOConnect offers.*

I am an accountant by trade originally. WAOConnect is designed to help companies find the right software system to run their product-based business on. About 95 percent of our customers use Shopify. Our business attracts clients that need systems to manage their inventory and all the operations of their business that relate to inventory. We help our clients understand how to manage their inventory successfully if they're a product-based business.

Q: *When it comes to inventory management, what are some of the biggest mistakes you see startup Shopify-based ecommerce businesses making?*

Many companies start up with absolutely no inventory-management system in place. The company starts to grow quickly because they have one or more successful products, but with no inventory-management system in place, even if it's a paper-based or spreadsheet-based system, the company quickly starts experiencing problems knowing whether they have enough product to fulfill demand. This often results in experiencing customer-service issues as a result of not being able to ship products in a timely manner.

Proper inventory management can help prevent a company from having a back-order status, which could result in losing customers. The problems become even greater if the company is selling the same product across multiple sales channels beyond just Shopify. Understanding what your sales rates are as a business operator will help you determine when to acquire more inventory and how much inventory you'll need to meet demand, while keeping inventory-warehousing costs affordable.

Q: *When would you recommend that a startup company implement an inventory-management system?*

The natural journey of most Shopify startups is that they launch their company and start testing out the products they plan to sell. Once the business proves viable, putting an accounting and bookkeeping system such as QuickBooks into place is typically the next step for a growing business. At this point, the core inventory-management tools offered by Shopify and its accounting system should be adequate to meet the company's initial needs, assuming the company's operators take advantage of these tools in the proper manner.

Once a business starts selling multiple products online via their Shopify-based ecommerce website, as well as through multiple other sales channels, this is typically when a more powerful inventory-management system should be implemented, especially once the company starts having to manage its own warehouses.

Q: *How many products should an online merchant be selling before becoming concerned about adopting an inventory-management system?*

The number of products a company is selling is not necessarily a deciding factor. It's more a matter of how many units of a product are being sold, as well as through how many different channels they're being sold. We have had clients that developed huge inventory-management problems with just three products, but that company was selling through several different channels and handling its own manufacturing, so it also had to manage inventory for a bunch of raw materials, which would ultimately be transformed into its finished products, which then needed to be warehoused and sold. When a company needs to implement an inventory-management system is very much based on unique factors that pertain exclusively to their business.

Q: *For a startup business, what tips do you have related to accurate inventory forecasting, so the company never runs short on product to sell?*

You need to record and track everything about your business that's happening in real time. This will allow you to quickly draw on that information to make intelligent decisions. As soon as you know what your sales history is for a product, you can more accurately create a sales forecast and predict future sales and inventory needs.

Inventory Planner [https://www.inventory-planner.com/] is a software application that can help a small business with these projections, instead of having to rely on an Excel spreadsheet that you create and manage yourself. Even without an inventory system in place, the Inventory Planner application, or one like it, can be very useful to an ecommerce business when it comes to projecting future sales based on data about past sales and other factors.

An application like Inventory Planner will help you determine how much inventory you need to purchase and when, based on your sales history, the rate at which you're currently selling the product, your current inventory level, and what inventory has been purchased but not yet delivered. You also need to know how long it'll take you to receive new inventory once an order for it has been placed with your supplier, distributor, or manufacturer.

If you choose to handle inventory management using a spreadsheet, this is something your business will quickly outgrow, and for it to work from the beginning it needs to constantly be updated with the latest information and sales data, for example. As soon as you don't have time to manually update the information in the spreadsheet or you enter it incorrectly, you'll likely run into an inventory problem. An application such as Inventory Planner integrates directly with Shopify.

Q: *In your opinion, how good are the inventory-management tools offered by Shopify?*

Shopify offers basic inventory-management functionality that'll work initially for most startup ecommerce businesses, especially if you're not doing a lot of product bundling. Shopify's tool mainly offers inventory tracking. However, as of early 2022, it does not allow you to generate purchase orders for the acquisition of new inventory or manage inventory spread throughout multiple warehouses, for example.

Shopify acquired an application called Stocky [https://apps.shopify.com/stocky], which now comes free with a Shopify account, although additional fees apply to use it. It offers more powerful inventory-management functionality. If you're not doing any of your own manufacturing or operating multiple warehouses, the inventory-management tools offered by Shopify will be more than adequate, at least initially.

Q: *Do you have any advice about finding reliable product suppliers?*

While we are currently seeing all sorts of issues pertaining to the shipment of products, we rarely see ecommerce businesses having problems with their actual suppliers, especially if they've researched those suppliers and they're known to be reputable and reliable. The big problem companies run into is managing their inventory and knowing when and how much inventory to order from their suppliers.

It is essential that a business operator maintain detailed records related to all transactions with their suppliers and the performance of those suppliers, as well as their own company's operations. An ecommerce business operator needs to understand basic supply and demand issues pertaining to each product that's being sold.

Q: *How can a startup business deal with shipping-related problems that arise when it comes to ordering its inventory and fulfilling orders?*

There are some things that are just out of a small business operator's control. However, maintaining an open line of communication with your suppliers and the shipping companies you use will be very helpful and allow you to anticipate potential problems in advance. As soon as you know something is being delayed, you need to determine how that delay will impact your business and your customers.

If you have open communication lines with your customers, you can often appease them, so they don't cancel their order and wind up unhappy with your business. Honest communication with your customers is the best way to minimize any potential problems that arise from inventory-related delays.

Obviously, if you see inventory is taking longer to arrive at your warehouse, you need to order earlier than you normally would to help compensate for the delays. Don't wait until it's too late to properly manage your inventory or address delays that arise. At the very least, you need to keep your Shopify-related customer records up-to-date, so you know whom you've shipped orders out to and which customers are still awaiting order fulfillment.

Q: *Is there any other advice you can offer related to inventory management?*

Again, implement a system that allows you to record everything that's going on in real time, so that data can help you make the decisions you need to make. If you try to take shortcuts or go about inventory management in a haphazard way, you will not have the appropriate or accurate information at your fingertips to make the intelligent and financially responsible decisions that you need to make. As your business grows, your inventory management–related responsibilities will also grow, so it's important to be prepared. Start out with the right foundation, and understand what you need to do to manage your inventory accurately.

There's Still More to Consider

Instead of starting an ecommerce business from scratch, one of the few shortcuts you *can* take is to purchase and take over an already established business. The Shopify Exchange Marketplace, which you'll learn about in the next chapter, offers an online forum specifically for buying and selling existing Shopify-based ecommerce businesses.

CHAPTER 11

Consider Buying an Existing Online Business

You can easily spend weeks or months coming up with a great idea for an online business, finding products to sell, developing a website, and handling all the other tasks associated with launching an online business from scratch. An alternative to all that is to purchase an online business that's already fully operational and well-established.

One of the services that Shopify offers its users is the Exchange Marketplace (https://exchangemarketplace.com). Basically, it's an online forum for buying and selling fully operational ecommerce businesses on the Shopify platform.

The Benefits of Acquiring an Established Business

The 10 biggest benefits of purchasing an already operational business are:

1. You can save weeks or months by not having to plan, design, and launch your own ecommerce website.
2. Someone else has already found products to sell and sources to supply those products.
3. The website has an established brand and is already fully populated with product descriptions, photos, and other content.
4. The original business operator has pinpointed their target audience.
5. The business concept has proved viable and has an established customer base.
6. The original business operator already understands the competition.
7. The original business operator knows how to market and advertise the business to drive traffic to the site.
8. An accounting/bookkeeping system is already in place.

9. The business has been set up as a legal entity.

10. When you acquire an existing business, the seller can serve as a consultant or tutor to get you up to speed on how it operates.

Additional Considerations Before Taking Over an Existing Business

But before you jump in and buy an established ecommerce business, it's essential to do your research. Determine if the business is truly profitable and viable, whether it has long-term growth potential, and whether it's worth paying a premium for an established business (instead of creating a similar ecommerce business yourself from scratch).

The first question to ask the seller is why they're selling the business. Try to get the most detailed answer you can. Next, have the seller walk you through every step of the business operation. Have an independent accountant review the company's books and study the website traffic and conversion rate reports offered by Shopify and other analytics services.

Are the products the business sells still in high demand? Do you anticipate the demand will grow over time and the audience for the products will expand? Is it likely the products will become obsolete soon or that consumer trends will change and decrease demand for them?

Next, carefully evaluate how much competition the business is facing and to what degree that competition will pose a challenge to the success of the business if you take it over.

Even if the business looks great on paper and the financial records show it's a viable and profitable operation, really do some inner soul searching. Make sure it's a concept that you're truly passionate about and that if you buy the business, you'll be selling quality products you believe in. Also make sure the target audience for the business is one you understand, relate to, and know how to reach through advertising and marketing.

As you're evaluating the company's current state of operation, consider what you'd do differently to help it grow, and whether you have the financial resources and time to make the desired changes. Are those goals realistic, achievable, and in line with your own career and lifestyle objectives?

Of course, you also want to think about how you'd finance the purchase of the business, what additional expenses you'd have immediately upon taking it over, and how long it would take to recoup your initial investment. If you don't have a business finance background, consider working with an accountant to develop a strong financial plan for yourself and the business.

Once you express an interest in a business for sale, you'll have a chance to interact with the seller via a secure messaging system hosted by Shopify. During this initial communication, you'll want to learn as much about the seller and the business as possible, so have a list of questions ready.

Here are some sample questions to help you get the conversation with a seller started:

- Tell me about your background.
- What other businesses have you owned and/or sold?
- What made you initially start the business?
- Tell me about the brand and story behind the business.
- Who is the target audience for the business? How large is this audience?
- What's the history of the business?
- Why have you chosen to sell the business?
- What's been the most rewarding aspect of running the business?
- What's the biggest challenge you face keeping the business going?
- What pitfalls do you anticipate the new business owner will encounter?
- How much time do you spend running the business each week?
- How large and loyal is the existing customer base?
- Have you developed standard operating procedures for the business that you'll be willing to share?
- If I were to take over the business, how much initial support can I count on from you?
- In addition to Shopify reports, do you have third-party analytics that show the overall success of the business?
- How do you currently drive traffic to the website?
- What's the average conversion rate between site visitors and paying customers?
- Will you provide a comprehensive P&L statement as well as other financial records for me and my accountant to review?
- Where do you acquire your inventory?
- What is the cost of goods sold and gross profit?
- What are the company's operating expenses and what is its net income?

Discover What Shopify Exchange Marketplace Offers

Shopify's Exchange Marketplace is divided into categories for easy browsing; listings include established businesses and dropshipping websites for sale. The sellers are typically willing to work with the buyers to help them succeed when they take over the business.

Each business listing offers a preview that showcases a photo or company logo, the company's name, a short description of the business and what it does, and basic financial information (including average monthly revenue, average profit per month, inventory value, and the asking price). Just above the business name, look for a banner that says, "Offers Support." When you see this, it means the seller will be willing to work with you and offer training once you acquire the business. It'll be up to you to agree on the level, duration, and form this support will take.

Once you find a listing that interests you, click or tap on the View Listing button to see a much more in-depth summary of what the business does and its financials. This expanded description will tell you about the company's story, its founders, and give you an overview of what's involved with running the business. You'll also discover more detailed information pertaining to the company's financials and sales performance, with numbers verified by Shopify.

Shopify also reports revenue that it pays to the company's current operator, details about website traffic, a summary of Shopify-related business expenses, information about the company's current suppliers, and the size of the company's mailing list.

There's also a Seller's Advice section for each business listing, which offers the seller's perspective about how the new owner can grow the business and what skills they believe are necessary to successfully manage it.

The Benefits of Using Exchange Marketplace

Purchasing an established ecommerce business through Shopify's Exchange Marketplace, as opposed to through an independent business broker or by working directly with the seller, has its advantages. The biggest benefit is that because Shopify is the ecommerce platform used to operate the business, it can verify much of the information provided by the seller and pass along data to prospective buyers that the seller cannot modify.

Exchange Marketplace also features a secure messaging platform that buyers and sellers can use to communicate and offers an escrow payment system as well as a dedicated Shopify team that will help transfer the business from the old owner to the new one.

When an ecommerce business is listed for sale on the Exchange Marketplace, Shopify works with the owner to calculate an accurate valuation for that business. To help buyers understand the process of acquiring a business, Shopify offers a variety of online training materials and a free ebook, which you can download at https://exchangemarketplace.com/buy-a-website.

As buyers begin their search for the perfect business to acquire, they can search by business location, type, and/or industry, and then narrow down their search using filters such as selling price, average monthly revenue, time in business, and the industry the business focuses on. At any given time, thousands of ecommerce businesses are for sale on the Exchange Marketplace, so using these filters allows you to nail down your choices faster.

Throughout the business purchase process, and then once you acquire your new business, Shopify's in-house experts are available 24/7 to help you with a smooth transition, ensuring all the settings are properly adjusted and all relevant accounts are transferred to you.

In the end, whether you choose to start an ecommerce business from scratch on the Shopify platform or acquire a preexisting business that you plan to grow, incredible opportunities are available to you, assuming you're willing to put in the necessary hard work and dedication.

While purchasing a preexisting business will definitely save you some time, when you buy someone else's business, you're also accepting their vision for it and the story as to why the business was founded in the first place. The business already has a brand, reputation, and online presence, so it doesn't make sense to make drastic changes right away. If you don't agree with the vision, philosophy, and approach of that business, you may be better off seeking another opportunity or starting your own ecommerce business your own way.

Final Thoughts . . .

We're living in an exciting time in which technology plays a huge part in our daily lives—including how we buy the things we need. This has created a tremendous opportunity for entrepreneurs looking to establish and operate an ecommerce business, and while countless online tools can help you do this, few others (if any) offer as many features and functions as Shopify.

Hopefully, by reading this book, you've discovered that Shopify offers an incredibly powerful, relatively easy-to-use, and customizable platform from which just about anyone can operate a branded ecommerce business selling products to customers around the world in a cost-effective way.

It all starts with coming up with a great product to sell online, becoming truly passionate about the business you're planning to launch, doing your research, and discovering how to make full use of Shopify's ecommerce tools. As an entrepreneur, you'll also need to be patient, persistent, creative, and continuously focused on your objectives.

(Remember, though, that the Shopify platform is evolving as fast as the rest of the internet—and the buying habits of consumers—so you'll need to keep current with and take advantage of these latest technologies and trends.)

Yes, starting an online business can be a challenge, and it is risky. However, if you maintain realistic goals, your ecommerce website can also become a profitable business venture, and one that you'll love operating.

Have fun and good luck!

About the Author

Jason R. Rich (www.jasonrich.com) is an author, journalist, photographer, and public speaker who is an internationally recognized consumer technology expert. He serves as a consumer technology writer for Forbes Vetted (https://www.forbes.com/vetted/) and regularly writes about consumer technology for *AARP The Magazine* (www.aarp.org/magazine) and AARP.org, along with a variety of other magazines and websites.

As an author, he's written more than a dozen business-oriented books for Entrepreneur Books, including *Ultimate Guide to YouTube for Business* (Second Edition) and several guides in the publisher's *Start Your Own* series, including *Start Your Own Etsy Business* and *Start Your Own Podcast Business*. He's also had numerous books published by Wiley, Pearson/Que Publishing, Penguin Random House, McGraw Hill, and Skyhorse Publishing.

Throughout the year, Jason lectures about consumer technology aboard cruise ships operated by Carnival Cruise Line and others. He also teaches adult education classes throughout New England.

You can follow Jason on Facebook (https://www.facebook.com/JasonRich7), Instagram (https://www.instagram.com/JasonRich7/), Twitter (https://twitter.com/JasonRich7), and LinkedIn (https://www.linkedin.com/in/jasonrich7).

Index

CPSIA information can be obtained
at www.ICGtesting.com
Printed in the USA
JSHW011443290822
29834JS00001B/1

9 781642 011494